Mallee Roots

Bill Hampel

Mallee Roots

Acknowledgements

Thanks to Kerry my wife for her suggestions after reading an earlier draft. Thanks also to daughter Petra for her patient editing. I appreciated also the inspiration from Barry Revill's writing group and Trevor Matthew's helpful suggestions about the epilogue. Despite this very welcome help, the shortcomings are all mine.

Mallee Roots
ISBN 978 1 76041 662 1
Copyright © Bill Hampel 2018

First published 2018 by
Ginninderra Press
PO Box 3461 Port Adelaide 5015
www.ginninderrapress.com.au

Contents

From Farm to Post Office	7
A Bird's-eye View	12
People on the Fringe	18
Silo: Economic Hub and Landmark	26
Beyond the Main Street	31
Our House	37
Fruits of a Good Life	44
Voyage Around My Mother	53
Aged Grandparents and Their Children	65
Religion for the Non-believer	71
Non-pecuniary Diversions	79
Communing With Nature	84
The Perks of Being 'Disadvantaged'	87
Horizons Expanded	94
Primary School Had Its Challenges	102
A Father Who Made It Easy	111
The Exquisite Pleasure of Murray River Fishing	115
Induction Into the World of Adults	124
Not Friendless, but…	130
Farmer Speech Patterns and Behaviour	139
Budding Entrepreneur	142
Girls	149
The Last of the Knucklemen	153
Every Town Needs a Focus	157
Grief and Diversions	169
Secondary Schooling, a Process of Attrition	176
Epilogue	199

Walpeup

From Farm to Post Office

Silo Jack was very tall, like the silo he kept, but angular, even gaunt, a dusting of wheat dust on his black hat and bony cheeks. At first sight grim as an undertaker, with bent pipe in his mouth, he was anybody's friendly uncle. He told me not to get in the way of wheat trucks but was happy to have me hanging around. I waited patiently, chewing handfuls of wheat into dough, ready to ask carters for a ride on their next trip out.

I was glad I went home early that day. Dad told me what happened.

The late afternoon sun had lost its sting, the last truck had rumbled in, and paddocks had returned to dry spears of monotonous stubble. As he had done in years before, Jack mounted a barrel of beer on the back of a truck in the shadow of the silo. Their carting season over, carters and farmers were ready for a drink. The silo keeper's gesture didn't surprise me. In a tiny country town like mine, generous acts like this were common enough. The problem was that this time, things didn't work out as intended.

Often, a few locals took advantage of Jack's hospitality. He was happy with that, but I'm told things got out of hand. Beer slowed to a trickle, and agitated voices bounced up the sheer face of the silo. Differences of opinion magnified, ancient slights surged, and with Silo Jack's entreaties falling on deaf ears, the once convivial occasion descended into a fistfight. The evidence next morning of this undignified chaos was all too apparent.

It was unsettling when I heard what happened at the silo and witnessed its aftermath. As a kid, I found Walpeup grown-ups friendly; I felt comfortable with them. Just as well, because there weren't many kids my age in town.

Next morning, a Saturday, cars lined the main street for shopping. Farmers chatting, probably the usual topics: family, crops, sheep and football. Not many grumbled about the hostile climate. Pessimism was not an option. This time, conversations had a special flavour. When several men sported black eyes, the street buzzed with a mixture of humour and curiosity. As usual, they wandered into the post office with a perfunctory 'Any mail, Ivan?' to my father, the postmaster, then settled in for an amiable chat.

Silo Jack emerged unscathed from the fracas at the silo. Others, farmers, Jack Hennessey and Jack Smythe, either cautious drinkers or just lucky, also bore no imprint of the chaotic event. I was glad that Jack Hennessey did not take up the challenge. He served a tennis ball like a whirling dervish and I'd seen him pounce across the court like a mountain lion. Others weren't so lucky. Jack Wallace (or Farmer Jack as he was called), stationmaster Jack Ensleigh (or Railway Jack) and garage mechanic Jack Freeman (or Hydraulic Jack) all showed evidence of their contribution to the stoush. Even I could read discomfort on their faces.

By afternoon, though, everyone seemed to see the funny side. At heart, most knew that our silo was an important centre for brief social exchanges between farmers. Despite their being small-scale businessmen and competitors, it reminded them they shared an unpredictable climate and a shared destiny. What welled to the surface on that hot evening and provoked these normal peaceable men into violence, I wondered.

No question why farmers welcomed a refreshing end of season beer. It gets hot – or, as the locals would say, 'bloody hot' – in Walpeup. With the horizon a shimmering mirage, summer daytime temperature often hovered around forty degrees. Perversely, in winter, morning frosts crunching underfoot gave way to windless sunny days. By lunchtime, I could sometimes comfortably discard my school jumper. Rainfall was punishingly variable with an average of 341 millimetres. In 1944, it got down to six inches (179 millimetres) – well inside the reading for a desert.

The saving grace is that nights were a stargazer's heaven. We needed no persuasion to spend very hot ones on folding stretchers out in the backyard to catch every bit of breeze. I was never a very imaginative person but Mallee skies on a summer's night transfixed me. Against the Milky Way's incandescent carpet, piercingly white stars formed endless patterns, enough to keep us staring upward and wondering until sleep took over. When the light of a big moon suffused the sky, I was fascinated by the man filling one side of the sphere, arms outstretched above him, herding sheep. It was one of nature's perfect Rorschach tests.

In those early years, isolation and an agricultural system based on family farms sustained a strong community spirit. Economic change was already apparent but until I was nearly seventeen and left the district, the town was for me a functioning and comforting social and commercial entity. Especially in my early years it provided a store of rich experiences, undoubtedly more so for the freedoms granted boys.

Today, sitting in the semi-desert Mallee of Victoria's north-west, Walpeup only seems to get a mention in temperature reports on ABC television. Economic change has bypassed many such towns. They hang on: paint peeling, building repairs long overdue. The demise of others is marked by nothing more than broken concrete and greying pieces of wood projecting from the weeds. While bigger centres thrived, they lost out. Farmer has bought out farmer. Properties are now three times the size and rural areas correspondingly depopulated.

It might be asked why our family would pile into their Erskine in 1942 when I was three and leave the farm further west to come to such a place. But there was plenty of motivation to make the move. After being demobbed from the army in the early 1920s, Dad gave the farm his best shot for twenty years.

As older brother Ian revealed snippets of information about Dad's war experience and the privations of running a farm emerged, I found it hard it hard to reconcile them with his equanimity and often optimism. Farming west of Ouyen had been about enduring long days of mind-numbing physical toil. Horses to be fed, groomed and harnessed. Fences to be maintained. A channel dug by hand. Pigs to be fed and night soil buried. What Dad learned about extracting value from an undersized holding with poor soils in devilishly variable seasons, he learnt on the job. There were no visits from agricultural extension officers to fill in the knowledge gaps of former soldiers like him. He never spoke of the demeaning supervision exercised by government officials to ensure that such soldier settlers were doing their bit to justify receipt of the often inadequate government assistance.

There was no local Landcare group to provide a conduit to research, government grants for fencing, or the fellowship of other farmers. One neighbouring farmer even claimed – in fact robbed – some of Dad's sheep by rebranding them. Not content with this, he jammed the floater on our sheep trough so that our animals died of thirst. He then had the gall to ask Dad if he could 'just take those dead sheep (and their wool) off your hands'. My father made no report to the police, partly because of the difficulty in finding proof.

It never ceased to amaze my older brother Ian that he should see reason for optimism. But few could endure without having such an outlook. Ian, by contrast, saw no future in the farm's financial viability or his life on it. He hated the purposeless grind, so he elevated his age and enlisted in the army. Having thieves as neighbours wouldn't have enhanced the appeal to the farm's next buyer. It's easy to see why life as Walpeup postmaster appealed to my father.

Farm life until 1942 was no kinder to my mother. She had equal justification to leave. In above-century temperatures for weeks on end, she raised four children and, later, a young baby on a farm that lacked all amenities, particularly cooling and refrigeration. Tank water had to be sparingly used and reliance on a wood-fired kitchen stove added to stifling summer heat. Unprotected by shady trees and a veranda, relentlessly invaded by buzzing flies, and severely overcrowded, our weatherboard house and its surrounds deflated the spirits. Small comfort that this was the typical lot of many Mallee farmers' wives in the 1930s.

When I learnt of conditions on the farm, Mum's obsessive desire in later years to live in a solid brick house assumed new meaning. Apart from their appearance of permanence and solidity, brick homes are also generally cooler, at least for short heat spells.

To add to her burden, she also had to cook for one or more farm labourers. One of them, Charlie, came to visit us in Walpeup. Never the most exciting conversationalist, he was, as Ian put it, not the sharpest tool in the shed. He had a disturbing fixed stare and a very large dent in his left forehead, the legacy of a disgruntled horse's backward kick.

I was three when we left, or rather – if Ian's rejection of the life was a measure of family sentiment – happily abandoned the farm. The earliest recollection I have of Walpeup was that of a lone flickering candle burning on a kitchen dresser, shrouded voices, and the scraping of furniture being shifted.

A Bird's-eye View

Some things endure. Rising to forty-five metres, our wheat silo dwarfed the only other structures breaking the horizon, the two ageing water tanks mounted on the hill. Houses were all single-storey. For some town dwellers, the silo was just a couple of concrete cylinders with a galvanised roof that cast a late afternoon shadow over the main road. For us kids, it was a perpetual challenge to land a penny from the road onto its roof. Most often, the coin simply clattered and echoed disappointingly down the side.

A solid concrete structure like our silo, built in 1939, embodied promise of continued prosperity, but it was certainly not unique. Silos with more or less equal number of bins dotted the railway line running due west from Ouyen to Murrayville near the South Australian border. They were silent sentinels above the near-flat countryside and served as milestones for motorists trailing billowing dust as they journeyed along the only main road.

Spending so much time in the silo's shadow, I'd long had a desire to go up to the top and see what my town looked like from above. After all, there was no way we kids could shin up the fat poles supporting the two water tanks up on the hill. At first, Silo Jack said I was too young to make the climb. Finally, when I reached mid-teens, he relented. Any latent fear of heights was softened by the interior's division into ten storeys, concrete platforms, each linked by steel ladders. Step by step, rung by rung, my courage increased. At last, hands gripping each rung like an eagle with a rabbit, and the rasping sound of my feet reverberating up and down the darkness, I made it. I opened the door looking east from the galvanised iron hut at the top and cast my eyes over the brown and green of the Mallee flatness. Below, the township that once loomed so large and bounded the limits of my life, now looked like the model village at Bourton-on-the-Water we had seen in the English Cotswolds earlier that year.

We had three general stores lining the settled side of the road. Closest to the silo was Mrs Dickie's. If longevity is the measure, Mrs Dickie's store was worthy of distinction. Established in 1911, it was the first general store in town and one of the earliest in the Mallee. Unlike the original structure, it was now of brick, cool inside and, with limited merchandise to sell, its large display window was superfluous. It was its owner's practice to sell to needy kids liquorice that shattered in the hand, boiled lollies long past their use-by date, and all-day suckers that would have passed as archaeological specimens. This provocation was a challenge we were not going to shirk. We reacted to her stinginess by filching some of those on display, despite her watchful lurking up behind. She also stocked token wrinkled fruit and vegetables for those with no inclination to garden and not very discerning eyes.

Further along stood a very modest bakery, put to use by Mr McCurdy, just back from service as an army cook. Normally, to call an army cook a chef would be an oxymoron but not Mr Mac. His hot, golden flaky sausage rolls and small loaves of crusty bread (loafers as we called them) that he passed through a hole in our paling fence confirmed both his skill and generosity. A bonus was the primeval mouth-watering smells of baking bread wafting our way.

The savings bank further down the street staggered along on a part-time basis, served by an Ouyen branch until finally it closed. Its shutting up shop foreshadowed the departure of services from small country towns in years to follow. With the aim of promoting thrift, most kids were encouraged to keep a small Commonwealth savings box for coins. But the bank building did service to community in another way. On Sunday mornings, Lacey (Wallace) Caldwell and I sat on its concrete front steps to swap and read comics, always assured of quiet in Walpeup. We weren't bosom buddies; our relationship was one of mutual advantage. One of my favourite comics featured the hooded, muscular and invincible Phantom (the Ghost Who Walks). As with the other contemporary superhero, Superman, invincibility had a certain appeal for young kids. Second favourites were Blackhawk comics set in the Korean War. US jet pilots blasted North Korean War commies from the skies, miraculously without loss. For avid consumers of comics, it was good to be always on the winning side. Prose in these comics might not have owed much to elegance or rivalled that of Milton and Shakespeare, but at least we were reading something. There were few books available in our house or the community.

Mr and Mrs Kendrew occupied the bank residence at rear. Mr K reminded me of a cowering dog about to be chastised by its irate master for playing hide and seek with his gumboots. Perhaps it was just his age. He kept occupied mending the shoes of locals but there was surely another reason for his spending long hours out in the back shed. Mrs K earned the title of Radio 3WLP (our wireless was always tuned to ABC 3WV, western Victoria) because every titbit of information, no matter how confidential, hit the airways as soon as she heard about it. Most treated her transmissions with a measure of scepticism, but her self-appointed role as bearer of gossip spiced up her life considerably.

Further along the main road, Digger (he was a World War II veteran) ran a farm supply agency: machinery, fertiliser, petrol and other things of vital interest to people on the land. It was a business sustained by a still relatively closely settled agricultural community even though farmers had begun abandoning their properties not long after World War I. Life was just too tough, particularly for returning soldiers trying to eke out a living under the soldier settler scheme. This exodus began not long after the end of Mallee scrub rolling that had been more or less obligatory for new landowners to maximise the farming potential of their allocated land.

Digger's house, a converted billiard room, and business were next door to our second residence. The green felted tables and bended figures in half shadow under low hanging lights had had a real mystique for me. Who played? I wondered. I was sorry to see it converted to more domestic purposes. Digger sold petrol too. As summer's heat waned, and his store of forty-four-gallon petrol drums contracted in the evening chill, they emitted an endless percussive chorus. We never gave a thought to what would be left of us and the neighbourhood if a fire broke out among them.

Digger earned unquestioned respect not just as a returned soldier, but also for his personal qualities. Few in rural areas were untouched by war. With him, the war left no apparent scars, physical or mental. He seemed to combine a genial and generous nature with a capacity for speaking directly.

Local telecommunications at the time involved telephone party lines, connected at our post office and simultaneously linking the receivers on several farms. In an emergency, this had its advantages, but could be abused. Mrs Maxwell at the end of one of these party facilities enriched her day by eavesdropping conversations. Digger knew of her habit. One day, while hoping to speak to another customer, he asked Dad (who as postmaster, had connected him), 'Is that silly old bugger on the end of the line again?'

Dad heard a clunk of a receiver being hastily replaced.

Coincidentally, Digger's new wife, Ila, was the daughter of Dad's World War I friend along the Murray. Consistently cheerful, she had a hearty laugh, not the sort of nervous, uncontrolled outburst betraying a person lacking in confidence. A trained nurse, she stepped without hesitation into the role of surrogate mother for me and my brother Bruce while Mum had to spend some time in the Ouyen hospital. Bruce was just over three years my senior. Ila had not yet started her own family so this was new territory. I was intrigued and impressed that she was no slouch in arm wrestles with me. I should not have been surprised. At the time, nursing entailed its own bit of manual labour even before the nation's waistlines swelled to their current state.

On the other side of our house stood Simpson's modest grocery store, a distributing point for bread we delivered gratis to farmers with their mail. For our small service, they reciprocated with home-grown vegetables and fruit in season. Miss Simpson was a small, spectacled woman who never missed an opportunity to show she had a business to run. Despite her limited stock and competition for a small market with two other shops, her tiny store was destined to out-survive them.

Out the back, in full view from our kitchen, her nephew Simmo, his mind elsewhere, lifelessly transferred potatoes from hessian sacks to smaller paper bags for sale. A bit of a joker, and a good tennis player when he tried, but with little drive and no qualifications, word came that he later died prematurely of alcoholic poisoning. As always, loss of hope drains ambition and by no means was he the exception in the district. I would have loved to ride on his Matchless motorbike and tour around town like he did. His bike was his way of transcending small-town living. I rode the wheat trucks.

At the end of the street rounding out the town's retail activity was Landry's grocery and department store: cool brick, big blocks of cheese on the wide wooden counter, open bags of flour on the floor and, in white apron, proprietor who wore glasses pushed up over his wrinkled forehead. Landry's perpetually cool interior would sometimes tempt us to bypass Simpson's to sample some of its limited stock. The concept of general store seemed to know no bounds. Inspired by tales of legendary American woodsman Davy Crockett, I used my precious returns from dead wool and beer bottle sales to buy a hunting knife. About twenty-five centimetres long, it could have done real damage to any Indian brave I should come across in the wilds of Walpeup. Dad made me take it back, much to my disappointment and embarrassment. Although it wasn't Dad's intention to humiliate me, I finally saw the need to return it. It wasn't the last unwise purchase I made in my life but a lesson for me in decision-making. In retrospect, that was probably Dad's goal.

Of modest frontage, Sidney's butcher shop next door to Landry's had sawdust covering the floor and, for a chopping block, a huge sawn tree stub, girth many times bigger than any Mallee tree could produce. It must have been from a red gum and trucked in from along the Murray River. Hundreds of indented lines from multiple cleaver blows told its history of years of service. A measure of the amount of meat consumed locally was that two butchers were kept busy on Saturday mornings when farmers came to town. They worked well together in the cramped space although assistant butcher Billy Bent had to duck to avoid meat hooks hanging from the rail at the back. Many farmers killed their own but sought out Sidney's for variety. The butcher shop's meat came from animals they killed in slaughter yards over a kilometre away. In a high wind, its noxious odour of mud, dung and decayed blood wafted to the edge of town. Not totally without logic, as a little kid, I thought the slaughter yards were the snorty yards. After all, pigs also spent their last moments there too.

I had long hankered to see how the local butcher made the sausages we ate with mashed potato, peas and cabbage. Sausage production was a modest operation at the back of the butcher shop. Mr Sidney's flourishes suggested he was flattered by my interest. I stood at a respectable distance to watch bits of gristle and beef churned into continuous straws of malleable substance in a mincer five times the size the one we used at home for our rissoles. Lamb was the less popular ingredient for sausages despite massive consumption in other forms. I was fascinated by the steady, patient oozing into sheep's intestines threaded onto the mincer. The machine might have been much bigger but still had to be turned by Billy Bent's muscular forearms. As if engaging in a centuries-old craft, Mr Sidney applied regular pressure of index finger, thumb and a final twist to turn tubes of meat like a flexible pale garden hose into sausages. While their sausages said much for our butcher's manual dexterity, they said little for his desire to seduce the market. Somehow, their sausages always came in one standard thick variety and of one standard length.

People on the Fringe

Farmers had an accepted place in the community. They provided the base for the town's economy. Others played bit parts. One of these others, Kevin, a casual farm worker, lived for a short time in an abandoned farmhouse. His stay was as brief as my friendship with him, both cut short when I learned from Mum that he was charged with sheep stealing.

Kevin at least had a brief stake in the agricultural economy, but others were clearly fringe dwellers – on the margins of a town itself on civilisation's fringe.

Marmaduke sat shrouded by smoke of his campfire near the football ground. Alone, dirty trousers, broken-laced boots, wrapped in military great coat, his cheeks sunken and bewhiskered, he embodied hardship. He was part of a remnant army of Depression-era swagmen wandering across rural areas with roll of bedding or swag and billy for tea in search of odd jobs. Mum offered him one, chopping Mallee stumps. It was surely an act of kindness on her part because one of the regular chores for Bruce and me was to split along fault lines red and white Mallee stumps we burnt in kitchen and dining room. It would have been little comfort to a swagman like Marmaduke that the term had been immortalised in 'Once a jolly swagman camped by a billabong…' the first lines of 'Waltzing Matilda', long the sentimental Australian anthem first penned by nineteenth-century bard Banjo Paterson. This lone toothless swaggie had a harmonica as his constant companion, seeming to bring solace to his solitary and dismal existence.

Although curiosity drove me as I rode out to the footy ground to see him, I had a measure of sympathy for him. Some would doubt my sympathy and I put it down to peer pressure.

One day, on one of his infrequent visits to town, he wandered up from Mrs Dicky's towards the memorial hall. My mate Butchy Sidney, eager to test his newly acquired airgun, chose as his target Marmaduke's retreating backside. The victim wheeled around with stinging pain but shamefully, we did not hang around to confess to Marmaduke. (I should add that, strictly, Butchy was brother Bruce's friend because my hold on the handle of friendship with Butchy was shaky.)

About three kilometres out of town, there was another unexpected encampment of what were immediately identified with dread as gypsies. With horse and caravan, they had pulled in at the edge of a dam, our favourite place for tadpoles. Curiosity getting the better of me, I went too close. One dark, wrinkle-faced stranger grabbed hold of my bike – a crime for me about as bad as stealing a taxi-driver's cab. It was after all, the means of my mobility, my freedom and, occasionally, my income. I ran home to tell Dad, who immediately drove out from the comfort of our post office. I can still see him, raised to his full five foot eight, and in authoritative voice, cowing them into returning my livelihood. Again, to me, indisputable evidence that he was on my side. At that stage in my life, there were two camps: those with me and those against me, with little room for subtlety.

I had no proof of their ethnic origins, but I knew that neither precedent nor commercial interests of Afghans would prompt such action. Until this time, Afghans (in fact, mostly northern Indians) had an accepted place in the early 1940s economy, trading mainly cloth and items of clothing. We had many people of non-British origin in the district – mostly German – but ethnic origin most often simply didn't register. Rural areas were the last to be touched by the big post World War II influx of southern Europeans. Had the community seen greater cultural diversity, social and political conservatism might have had less of a stranglehold.

On the other side of the railway line in the shadow of the silo, we had the stationmaster, a couple of gangers (who undertook repairs along the line) and briefly a porter, but extra work required occasional extra labour. At this stage, 'gang' had no criminal connotations for me. It just meant a group of labourers. One of them, a dark-skinned bloke, probably around twenty, lived briefly in a railway van parked there by a goods train. Each summer evening for a few months, he came over for a chat with me, freshly bathed, a waft of deodorant, and black hair neatly slicked back with Brylcreem. For me it was of no consequence that he was an Aborigine – if I was even aware of it. I was pleased he thought me worthy of his company. We just chatted.

One who lived literally on the town's margins in the scrub was Dave Rowan. His dark skin should have registered with me but another feature took my attention. Every time I passed his tent fronted by its blackened bucket, pots, residual smell of campfire smoke and yesterday's cooking, and horse tethered nearby, Dave would say, 'Gday Bill' in a voice rivalling Paul Robson's in its depth and resonance. Even if the conversation went no further, I found the greeting comforting. Despite the depth of his voice, I never heard him launch into song. I did occasionally see him dance.

In the absence of income from social services, Dave trapped rabbits. Before the advent of myxomatosis in 1950, he did so very successfully. Every Saturday morning, his horse-drawn cart laden with his catch – now stiff with rigor mortis, gutted and strung in pairs over sticks running crosswise – bounced down to the local butcher's. From there, one of the two butchers drove him and rabbits to the freezer in nearby Underbool. Money in hand, he spent the afternoon in the pub 'pissing his earnings up against the wall', as was the expression. Then, still quite drunk and getting a lift home, he ambled down to dances in the memorial hall where men plied him outside in the surrounding scrub with yet more beer. His only dancing was an inebriated jig at the hall's entrance at the edge of a group of men mustering up the courage to ask girls for a dance.

I was conscious of Dave's Aboriginality, more so than with the young bloke visiting briefly as a railway employee. Yet I had no insight into what it was like to be marginalised in such a way. My family were not the source of any racist attitudes. If anything, they had pity for people like Dave – in retrospect, a not very helpful emotion. I recall no discussion about the historical legacy and structural elements of racism. Schooling failed to apprise us of Aboriginal people's centuries of prior occupation, except in brief, superficial, romanticised terms. What Dave did display was the problem of alcohol that figured prominently in the nation's past, especially on the goldfields in the 1850s and thereafter.

Alcohol was an issue in Walpeup. At some stage, I realised I had three choices: I could get married, as one girl of my age did before I finished high school; I could hit the grog; or I could get out. For me, the third was the only viable option, albeit not one made with great consideration.

Unlike many of his World War I compatriots, Dad didn't drink, nor did his eldest son, Ian. From my parents, messages about the demon drink tended to be implicit rather than explicit, more an expression of the toll it was taking on some men. Either women were cupboard drinkers or they had not succumbed to its charm, but booze was men's territory. Curiously, my primary school teacher, a known beer drinker, put before us a form from the Temperance Society on which we were to sign the pledge. No more than ten years old, I indignantly refused to comply, what some might see as an early sign of a spirited rebellion against authority and probably one the teacher should have anticipated. Children can be good at identifying hypocrisy.

While it is not recommended, a way of encouraging the postponement of alcohol consumption is to allow young boys to take a swig of port wine (threepenny dark) left in a bag outside the hall where a Saturday night dance had taken place. Bruce and I thought we would try it and did our best to conceal symptoms of our mysterious sickness for the rest of the day.

More widespread than its effects on my friend Dave on the fringes, the ravages of alcohol hit a number of young men in the community who killed themselves in motorbike or car accidents, fell off the back of a truck, or simply slid into death from alcoholic poisoning. City dwellers might have drunk as much, but it's plausible that such self-destructive behaviour in our district was not only in plain view but a pain-numbing response to boredom and emptiness. The effectiveness of my parents' stance on alcohol – if that was their intention – is debatable.

Carl Altman was one Walpeup identity I never met, mainly because he never emerged from his encampment in the Sunset scrub north of town. Who knows if he really had been in the German army as was rumoured? This hearsay made me more conscious of his ethnic or national origins, particularly given our family name and his first name being that of my late uncle Carl. A certain amount of mystique surrounds those who are different and unseen, and Altman inherited some of that intrigue. The only visitor to his bush home was Billy Bent, the butcher, who supplemented Altman's alleged diet of crows with a weekly ration of meat. I never learned how the reclusive individual got crows from tree to plate because there was no mention of a firearm. I had suspicions about that story. He did have his priorities right, however. On one visit, seeing his trousers worn with holes, Billy took him out a new pair. Next visit, Billy found that the bush dweller had used them to patch the old ones.

Mr Pit lived opposite Dave Rowan in a Spartan white cottage sitting like an elevated sentry box at the edge of a graveyard of rusting differentials, gearboxes, axles and radiators. I figured that the rambling workshop opposite must have once housed a thriving engineering business. As a matter of course, when I rode past Mr Pit's place looking for the cow, he would enquire about my schooling. Certainly his interest, his speech and his measured delivery – surprising, I thought, for a Scot – implied a more than minimal education or at least a traditional respect for it in his native land. That he was also a returned servicemen gave him automatic status in my eyes.

Among the abandoned motor parts, Mr Pit kept several beehives and, curiously to me, attributed all sorts of wondrous benefits to the honey that his rounded cheeks and rotund body suggested he consumed in large quantities. Rationalisation or not, he evidently had a sweet tooth. I used to see him down the street, carrying his groceries in a sugar bag slung over his shoulder as back straight, he bounced along from shop to post office. Although very much older than my sister Fay, he displayed a coy interest in her. She responded politely and a little amused.

One summer in my restless search for extra income, I became his employee in his workshop, where two naked light globes dangled over his cluttered workbenches. He asked me to take hold of a micrometer and measure what were thin slices of metal called shims – vitally necessary, he said, for a piston to function. An advance on my earlier task cleaning a carburettor, my complete ignorance of mechanics was compounded by a congenital lack of manual dexterity. Even replacing the chain on my bike stretched my capabilities. He stood two metres away, trying to conceal his incredulity that anyone could be so incompetent. Little did I realise that the money he paid me was not for any work I did. He just wanted company.

Out back lay Mr Pit's big project, a boat, perhaps a throwback to his previous life in the Tyneside shipyards. This was no humble tinny but a torpedo-proof welded steel vessel tough enough for service as a polar icebreaker. Happily, he had the foresight to build it sitting on a sturdy trailer attached to an old Buick tourer. With canvas hood, big headlights and additional dicky seats, his ostentatious vehicle sat oddly in contrast beside a terminally ill workshop. The Buick bespoke a genteel era. It evoked an image of upper middle-class women in pleated dresses and perky bonnets and men in spats, waistcoats and slicked down hair having an alfresco lunch on the grass beside their vehicle. Mr Pit had more practical motives in mind. He had his sights set on a launch at the newly filled and named Walpeup Lake sixteen kilometres away. My role was about to change from assistant mechanical engineer to ship's second mate.

This lake was dear to me. After all, ignoring the edict of not working on the Sabbath but with missionary axe-wielding zeal, I had helped Dad, Bruce and other Walpeup residents to clear the dead Murray pines from a natural depression. This was to be the much-anticipated lake, capturing surplus water from the Grampians that serviced farms and towns throughout the district. It became a very special place for people where the only other surface water was in dams for stock. Secretly viewed as interlopers, residents of Ouyen and beyond flocked there to join Walpeup people on hot weekends. As a long-standing resident, Mr Pit had the right to enjoy the fruits of our labour. As he drove his lovingly maintained vehicle south along the winding gravel road, his face had an intensity I'd not noticed before.

We took the track through the pines ready to launch his creation on its maiden voyage. Initial attempts to line the trailer up weren't successful. Perversely, as he tried to back it, it headed in the opposite direction with each turn of the steering wheel. Eventually, he managed to position it ready to launch at the top of a moderate slope. Moderate it may have been, but unhooked, and impelled by the icebreaker load, the trailer gathered alarming speed, threatening to cut a swath through the Murray pines as it charged towards the lake. No champagne bottle across its bows, it hit the water with a splash that sent startled ducks, cormorants, galahs and crows fleeing into the sky, their cries echoing across the silence. How come something so heavy – all that eight-millimetre steel – didn't plummet to the bottom? I wondered. To this point, science was absent from my school curriculum and even later in my final contact with it, Intermediate General Science A (Form 4 or Level 10 today), studied as a fourteen-year-old, Archimedes didn't feature. The water was at its shimmering and clear best. Contented picnickers' last sounds had melted into the trees and mud stirred up by children's gambolling and frolicking on inflated tubes the previous weekend had settled. Now only a zephyr rippled the lake surface. My captain leant back on his oars, his face creased in a faint lingering smile as we moved slowly along in the dappled shadow of bordering trees.

Mr Pit, like a number around Walpeup, led a fairly lonely existence.

He seemed to have few customers for his workshop, and the occasional shy but unsuccessful advances to my sister Fay, many years his junior, indicated he would have liked a companion. It would have been to cross a big age and cultural barrier for me to ask if he had ever had a companion. It was unrealistic to imagine that I could offer him very stimulating conversation, but remote places do tend to bring together people not usually seen as like minds.

Silo: Economic Hub and Landmark

For the farming community, the silo was a symbol of economic survival, the hub of a wheel of economic activity that radiated for miles around. Each summer, sweating growers and hired carters hauled wheat in bags and tipped it into the waist-high concrete hopper. A few carted in bulk. Pulled in over the grate between hopper and silo, they withdrew the hatch beneath the tray to let wheat hiss out – all over in minutes. Behind me, I could hear rumbling motors lifting the grain aloft in a chain of bushel-sized buckets into huge bins. From there, Silo Jack directed it into canvas-topped railway trucks lined up on the other side. All part of a routine, uneventful but an important activity for the community. Filling trucks, recording wheat density and chatting to carters filled Jack's day. If his cheerfulness was any guide, he seemed to find it fulfilling enough to return next season. Carting did not last forever. I had no idea what Jack did during the winter.

Antiquated Chevs, De Sotos and Fords jerking to a halt at the silo helped to relieve the boredom of my summer school holidays. Jack Smythe's ageing Ford still served him well even though its uneven chugging, Dad told me, indicated it was not firing on all six cylinders. Even though his belt now hung in an arc beneath his stomach, Jack took carting in his stride. Two bag hooks in hand, he would mount the tray behind his forty bags of wheat. Claws inserted, knees digging in, spine bent back, he dragged, pushed and kneed each 180 pounds across the tray to the hopper. With last grains sprinkling downwards, he pulled hooks out, sank one in the end of the bag, gave it a quick shake, threw it empty onto the pile and left. There was a practised rhythm about the process, nothing uncontrolled, every move part of a pattern. As he showed, for most physical tasks, the challenge was to use energy efficiently. A short stop at the weighbridge to weigh the empty truck and Smythy drove out to get another load. He was carting for himself so I supposed it was not worth his splashing out on a new vehicle.

I spent a lot of summer riding the wheat trucks. Perpetually chewing on wheat, I was patience personified. When another farmer or itinerant carter's unloading was almost complete, I would sidle up to ask if he was bringing in another load and if I could go out with him. With each, the driver worked alone, so I figured the risks from a knock-back were minimal. While never conscious of my motives, I saw riding a truck as a chance to explore surrounding roads, a way of expanding the environment of our tiny town. Perhaps influenced by my father, I liked to chat, to learn more about other people. I also wanted to feel useful and, I suppose, to feel accepted.

The advantage of bulk carrying was not lost on some, and novel solutions appeared. One or two were home-made galvanised iron constructions and some bigger, more substantial ones, were clearly the product of a manufacturer down south with an eye to the future. One who did own one of these futuristic devices was Andy Barrage. His was a World War II Blitz Buggy reincarnated as a bulk wheat carrier. I leapt at his invitation to join him. On the first of these trips, with the empty truck weighed at the weighbridge, we headed through the station yards and south on the gravel road. No road around Walpeup was sealed. Heat in his cabin was stifling, but an occasional crosswind wafting through the open windows relieved the smell of oil and sweat. I can still feel the burning from the engine cowling on the backs of my legs below my shorts, but I didn't dare say anything. Andy flicked sweat dribbling down his nose. Leg sinews taut, he double-clutched, changed down, and swerved around another pothole. Engine noise and the empty tray rattling behind us made conversation difficult. Andy took a long draw on his cigarette and gazed in silence across the golden stubble as we passed by now harvested crops. Apart from the noise, I found it hard to start conversation because he wasn't a local and I didn't know him well.

Now in my teens, once we arrived in a paddock, I took off my sandshoes. My task was to mount the near-full load of wheat and stumble across the top to reach the loader. I liked the tickle of wheat grains on my feet. As soon as Andy kneed the full bag on the loader and tripped the lever, the truck would give a lurch, lean slightly, then vibrate as loader and bag rose up in an arc like a cumbersome slingshot. I had to drag each bag, still a third full, off the loader, spread the wheat around, and hurl the empty bag below. To provide light relief, I would glide it as far as I could. After I had topped up the load by emptying several bags in this way, Andy would do a silent finger count of bags still standing and call me down. It was hard work and satisfaction modest, but I managed – an activity better suited to someone spending more time on fitness exercises and physical chores than reading books.

With loading finished, a simple pleasure was to slake my thirst from his dust-encrusted water bag. Passing air cooled it during its journey hooked to the front of the truck. I noted how Andy held the bag aloft along the back of his hand and forearm to direct water into his mouth. For me, still unskilled, an unscheduled face wash was a blessing in such conditions. Returning to town, he rewarded me with soft drink from Mrs Dickie's corner shop. Normally, soft drink didn't darken our family's doors. Bad for the teeth! Heaven knows, nature didn't need any help in that respect.

Silo Jack's job was to record wheat density in brass tubes suspended on what looked like scales. Weight per volume of each load must have been the basis of payment. He also watched with eagle eye for any sign of damp wheat. Silo Jack obviously enjoyed his brief chats with farmers and carters. No doubt these exchanges also achieved a bit of subtle quality control over the wheat they brought in. He had to take his job seriously. Any sign of wet wheat passing into the bins would have meant destruction of the entire contents, either from mould or spontaneous combustion, in either case a disaster for everyone.

There had been unseasonable summer rain and one day he ran grain from one of Bill Torrego's open bags through his fingers. He dipped his hand in again and with a gentle shake of his head said, 'Sorry, Bill. It's too damp. You know I can't let that stuff go into the bins.'

Torrego grumbled, hopped into his truck and left. I could see he wasn't happy.

Next load, he called the silo keeper over to the open bags of wheat. 'What do you think of this my friend? You're not gonna try it? Shove your hand in.'

Tentatively, Silo Jack pushed his hand in up to his wrist. Feeling something solid, he parted the grains to reveal a yabby arching its big front claw, a freshwater crayfish bred in local dams. Torrego had taken time out to net it and insert it in the bag, hoping it would not crawl out before he arrived at his destination. Luckily, this time his load passed the test.

Torrego had form. On another occasion when working for farmer Alf Turnitz, he heard the phone ring. He jerked the handpiece and its cord clean from the wall and took the useless phone, with cord dangling, to his employer in the next room. 'Someone calling for you, Alf.'

There was nothing subtle about country humour – potatoes shoved into car exhausts so that the engine would not start, a bit of decaying sheep left under the car bonnet on a hot truck engine, spark plugs swapped, grievances settled occasionally with fists – the default language of humour, anger or revenge in the district was action. Families lived by deeds, not words.

Either Silo Jack detected my desire to be useful or he was in his nurturing mood. Maybe he just wanted to see how this fourteen-year-old would react. We were standing next to one of the indestructible steel railway trucks nearly three metres high shunted into position beside the silo. I reckoned that, empty, they were as heavy as five of our Ford V8s and at first glance immoveable, especially when full of wheat. With pulse quickening, I stared at the pinch bar he used to shunt them along the railway line. It looked like a crowbar we used for digging post holes but with a bend on the end, and lots heavier.

After lying in the sun, the pinch bar was almost impossible to hold. He demonstrated how he wedged it under the wheel and, with both hands on the end, pushed down. Pressing until my feet left the ground, to my surprise, the wheel started to turn. Six times I pressed and slowly, the truck gathered speed and rumbled down the line until it exploded with body-shaking noise into its fellow trucks. Nerves settled, I now felt both useful and powerful. I looked around to see Jack smiling.

My other very direct contact with the railways came with the chance to ride on a steam engine, the sort used for wheat transport. I harboured no burning desire to be an engine-driver but, by far, no other machinery in the district matched a railway engine for size and power. Even for the mechanically ignorant as I was, demonstrations of power fascinated me. How could I not be curious to see what it I was like riding in a steam engine? After all, a train's arrival was a major event. I called up to the driver leaning one arm on the window as it idled and he readily obliged. Not many diversions in their work, I guessed. My ride was short, just the length of the shunting line. I also decided that shovelling coal through the small round hole into a glaring inferno was too much like hot, hard work, even in winter. On the plus side, this small journey forged a connection with the D3 steam engine we often saw out the kitchen window.

A few days later, a D3, its brakes squealing, hissed to a stop in the siding. It inched forward and, with a series of loud bangs like mechanical hand claps, the line of trucks linked up ready to be pulled away. I was told its destination was Geelong silos and then for export. Our railway line from Ouyen to Pinnaroo across the South Australian border had been laid down in 1919 specifically for this role. It was a lifeblood for both Mallee economy and community, no doubt reaching its historical peak with a fourteen-year-old's short-lived jaunt, shunting a truck along Walpeup track.

Beyond the Main Street

In front of the shops, a raised gravel road or highway ran westward to Murrayville, a town I can't recall ever visiting. While apparently not worth a trip, it assumed special status as the birthplace of my four siblings and me. On the other side of the road by the highway in Walpeup lay the plantation of sugar gums fenced off with the ubiquitous number 8 wire. These trees were well established, but in 1940s primary school, we small kids had a hand in establishing another plantation, also of sugar gums, nearer the school, perhaps continuing the local tradition where previous small kids had left off.

The impact of my thirteen years in Walpeup extended far beyond the years. It seemed much longer. During that time, the fence opposite our post office never had a gate. This puzzled me. Perhaps such a major infrastructure required application in triplicate to go to a railways bureaucracy nearly 500 kilometres away. A gate did not seem beyond imagination, especially for an almost direct route from post office and shops to the station. Cases of fruit – brought by train to meet Mum's inexhaustible desire to fill her Fowler's Vacola jars – were carried on Dad's shoulder and squeezed through the wires.

Soon after 1945, these wire strands came to serve the same purpose as today's roadside safety cables. Ian, returned from active war service, was reversing our powerful '39 Ford V8. Much like his younger brother, inclined to apply vigour where subtlety is required, he pushed too hard on the accelerator. The car rocketed out the driveway, roared over the road and, momentarily airborne, it descended the highway's sloping edge and came to a halt against the fence. When Dad raced over, he was relieved to see that the chastened driver remained unhurt.

Characteristically, Ian laughed off the episode partly because hitting a vehicle passing along the highway was unlikely.

Four poles spaced at eighty-metre intervals in front of the sugar gum plantation fence provided the only street illumination. Their dim light, pulsating with the irregular chugging of Bertie Connell's engine, its lone sound reaching across the night stillness, spread feebly towards the shops. Activity along the main thoroughfare was hardly brisk, so there was never cause to complain. When shops were shut, I found Bertie's engine comforting, a certainty that life went on in the darkness. Bertie also supplied electricity to the Memorial Hall.

Lining the railway line beyond the plantation, loomed a large goods shed, painted in regulation railway buff and brown. It was the only wall against which I could practise my tennis serves, even if the gravel space in front demanded more than reasonable agility. An almost complete absence of public buildings in town meant that any that did exist commanded my attention. The goods shed did indeed store goods in the form of bagged oats. Where there is bagged grain, there is usually grain spilt, and where there is grain in the offing, there are mice. One summer, at the height of a mouse plague, Bruce and I went looking for something to do and lifted the last empty bag from a pile. The rectangle of writhing, scurrying grey fur split asunder and exploded like shrapnel to the nearest corner. At home, while traps never sat idle, mice were simply of nuisance proportions. There also had to be some benefit from the numerous cats that gave birth, howled in ecstasy or agony in the depths of night and, as evidenced by the nauseating smell, died under the house.

The railway station rivalled the silo as a hub of activity, if on a modest scale. During the war, for example, it witnessed a joyful homecoming of troops on leave, spilling out of the dog box carriages to cover the platform. In the early 1950s, in addition to the stationmaster, Bobby Wilson, about eighteen, got a job as a railway porter, complete with hat and jacket. No one else wore a uniform in town and to me, in a tiny settlement with no discernible marks of status except stationmaster, it seemed a tad ostentatious. What on earth was he was going to do? I wondered. There are only so many times that fire buckets need to be refilled and brass lamps polished. Moreover, the task of exchanging a baton with passenger or goods train that might only pass through once a week did not seem to constitute a full job description. What was the point of this ritual reminiscent of an Olympic relay? Today, not even the station still stands. At that time, Walpeup had three houses for railway employees (Bobby lived elsewhere) in addition to mobile accommodation for occasional extra trackwork.

Apart from railway houses and houses attached to the row of shops in the main street, there was a wooden boarding house, or coffee palace as we called it, at the top end of the main street, opposite the silo. For a period in the forties, employees at the Mallee Research Station and other shorter-stay itinerant workers found accommodation there. It was two storeys nonetheless, and the last the town would see. The coffee palace was pulled down by 1950, at which point Mallee Research Station employees began living at their place of work several kilometres from town. Its trained officers engaged in its cereal breeding and planting trials and work on soil conservation. In the provision of labouring work, and the contribution of its field officers to the social and sporting life of the town, the MRS was hugely important. Wandering domestic turkeys decided that the coffee palace's now exposed partially filled cellar was a fitting place to lay their eggs. They made wonderful ammunition for juvenile warfare, but a direct hit was to be avoided at all costs.

Behind Walpeup's small commercial centre and accompanying residences lay about twenty homes, all with galvanised roofs creaking in desiccating summer sun and drumming to all too rare rain storms. The street from Mrs Dicky's corner led up past the Memorial Hall, to Mount Walpeup, a full 100 metres above sea level. At such an astronomical height, it was an obvious location for the town water supply, the aged, leaking pair of water tanks, heavily patched with tar and mounted on large knotty timber poles. To us, going past on our bikes, their wind-borne spray was a brief and welcome air conditioner. Water arrived there from a town dam served by long channels from southern Grampians storages or, to give its full name, the Wimmera-Mallee Stock and Domestic Reticulation System.

Further south, down the hill, hidden by scrub, sprawled the town rubbish tip. The tip was totally without order; people just dumped anywhere along the winding track dividing it whenever they lost the inclination to travel further. Discarded material included ashes from open fireplaces or, if misfortune struck, the sad remnants of a house fire. After Bertie Connell's house burnt down, it was sheer luck that Bruce and I began fossicking in his pile of ashes and unearthed a bounty of silver coins. Probably representing no more than his beer money, they had no heirloom value to us to warrant anything more than immediate spending. We could now supplement our weekly shilling pocket money with our favourite Cadbury's Old Jamaica chocolate, the closest I ever got to consuming rum.

To the east of the town, a gravel road crossed the railway line and swung sharply towards Ouyen. The crossing included a cavity over which spanned fifty-centimetre-thick beams for the railway line. For us town kids, it was a badge of honour to climb under the rails' supporting beams while a goods train hissed and rumbled its way overhead.

To the north of Walpeup, past the railway station, lay the three gypsum tennis courts. An annual rainfall of 340 millimetres ruled out lawn tennis. Their gypsum surface (calcium sulphate), a conglomerate of powder and shiny crystals, generated a fierce glare in bright sunshine, especially in summer. At least the glare encouraged observance of the rule to water before and after playing. In the Christmas school holidays, for Bruce and me, one game followed another except when duty called and we had to go inside to bottle fruit.

The courts were the scene of a tournament drawing competitors from as far as Mildura over 100 kilometres away. One visiting player of gorilla proportions had a crushing serve and menacing surge to the net. Dictated by custom as well as strength, women engaged in more sedate baseline rallies. Well-organised, the tournament also meant free soft drink for us ball boys from an ice-filled half-forty-four-gallon drum set among the bordering Mallee scrub. Everyone had a stake in the success of the event. Gertie Lander was especially generous, and while I had not yet learnt how to respond graciously to such kindness, any discomfort I felt did not stop me from accepting her kind offers of soft drink. As I got older, Sunday social tennis seemed to me to be a less benign affair. Somehow, veteran players managed more games on the roster than I did. Not a blatant manipulation, it seemed, just a gentle assertion of social power. Still, if this was the extent of social discrimination, I had few worries.

Leaving the tennis courts, the road, also gravel, continued past a large dam. Any body of water was worth a try. Such was the lure of fishing for me that I understood why cartoons showed kids trying their luck in a bucket. No trees bordered this dam to provide the shade that I knew fish liked but I thought I'd try anyway. One Sunday, I was so totally absorbed in watching for any telltale quivering in my line that I was oblivious of the sun's scorching heat. For one born in the area, it would seem obvious that the capacity of summer sun to do serious damage to one's skin was one of those life challenges I should have thought about. Still, we rarely wore hats, and sunscreen was unknown. Moreover, what could be a greater thrill than this? I caught several fish and as quickly as I landed them, I baited my line and cast out again. Finally, they stopped biting.

I pedalled home triumphant, bag of redfin pulling on my neck but disturbingly aware that the skin on my back was getting tighter and stinging more and more. Indoors, I peeled off my shirt to reveal massive sunburn blisters emerging that my mother likened to mini-saucers. The then popular treatment, liberal coatings of cold tea, produced an attractive tan like copper parchment with no observable healing potential. Reports were that lashings of butter, the other recommended treatment, weren't any better. This small lesson about sunburn had its sequel later on.

Finally, on its journey to our friends, Colman's farm, past the dam, the road diverted into the Research Station. Staff there conducted field days to display the latest trials of new species of wheat, barley and oats. Farmers in felt Akubra hats would mill around, keen to hear the results of the latest agricultural research. Besides the pursuit of better yields, trials were designed to combat ball smut and flag smut, virtually the only smut of either plant or human source that we heard about. In early primary school, the teacher of our one-teacher school took us to a field day, perhaps to give himself a break. As six to eight-year-olds we sat chatting in the early springtime sun on a carpet of capeweed alongside rows of wheat trials, threading daisy chains while we received serious instruction in the arcane science of plant breeding and fertilisers. Speakers had no amplification and up on a dray platform, their voices often carried off in the wind.

The MRS was the workplace of a succession of agricultural field officers I understood to be tertiary trained. Two of them were would-be suitors for my sister Fay in a district where the choice of partners was meagre and the gene pool small. Obligingly, one of them, in his desire to stake his claim, and assured of a no-contest from one so young, consented to an arm wrestle with me. What annoyances a suitor will endure! Arthur, one of the researchers but not a suitor, was a good footballer and there is no greater gift an incomer can offer to a country town than to inject talent into its footy team. Whether they are good at their chosen profession is of secondary importance. This also applied to teachers.

This then was the geography of my existence for thirteen years from an unremembered first three years of farm life further west until, at nearly seventeen, I left for university. Devoid of much intellectual stimulation, and with limited social activity, life in this small Mallee town still offered a wealth of experience and early responsibility for any young boy. Girls roamed less and, by permission and inclination, did fewer silly things, not that I thought about it much.

Our House

Custom and modest income dictated that our first house was small. Ten squares (each one hundred square feet) at most, it was built of wooden boards and large sheets of brittle material euphemistically called cement sheets that, in the light of current knowledge, were probably asbestos. A roof made of the ubiquitous corrugated galvanised iron amplified the pleasure of all too infrequent rains. Rooms were tiny, the largest space per person being the cement sheet and fly wire sleepout, the bedroom for Bruce and me. Rather than bedtime reading, we made up stories. Strangely, many seemed to feature flies. Perhaps it had something to do with the fact that, in summer, millions of small bush flies tried to sup in our eyes or scrounge for salt on our backs. The need to keep waving them away gave rise to the expression 'bush salute'. Less numerous were blowflies whose presence circling around any available meat sent housewives into frenzied defensive warfare. (Word has it that Walpeup was a corruption of an Aboriginal word meaning blowflies, a story that sounds to us suspiciously like something concocted by an Ouyen resident.)

Given the small size of our house, wall space was limited. However, Dad's brother Carl was an artist of note, if of a fairly traditional kind. Family legend was that the Queen held one of his paintings in her collection along with a couple of country galleries. Five adorned our walls. One was a scene of Pine Plains some distance south-west of town. What I could not understand was the inclusion in the landscape of a large expanse of water, allegedly from a flood. An infrequent occurrence in a region of such minimal and uncertain rainfall, I thought. That was until I saw a photo of my father paddling a raft somewhere in a 1920s' Mallee flood.

Although my uncle was obviously skilled, his trees troubled me. In

Dad rafting on 1920s flood.

their large size and dense foliage, they seemed more like European ones in higher rainfall areas I saw while abroad in 1953. My uncle, his wife and one son were killed in the 1942 London Blitz. Dad's painting skills were restricted to house improvement.

One other image, a print, not a real painting, hung in my parents' bedroom. Its grey blues and deep shadows haunted me when at early primary school age, I was confined to their bed with illness. My eye dwelt on the thin shafts of light hitting the helmets of soldiers pulling back on the reins of their rearing horses. My parents never explained its historical significance and I could not understand why they would want such a gloomy print in a room that was never well lit anyway.

Apart from kitchen stove and lounge room open fire, we had neither heating nor cooling, not even a fan. Without refrigeration, town dwellers and farmers alike depended on a Coolgardie safe to protect against flies and reduce food deterioration in summer's heat. Ours consisted of a steel frame covered in hessian, topped by a galvanised tray about two inches deep filled with water. Strips of Dad's retired flannel underwear draped down the side enabled water to seep from the tray through the hessian. Passing breezes increased evaporation and created cooling, a principle well-known to the Moors of equally hot Spain in medieval times. A legacy of the Depression and what I never fully realised was the deprivation of life on the farm, was that Dad felt nothing – including his long johns winter underwear – should be discarded. One of his favourite expressions was 'It might come in handy one day.' Regrettably, too often that day never eventuated and objects of questionable use seemed to accumulate in our garage.

Until we moved further along the street to the new post office location, we ate and did our school homework by the light of flickering and smoking kerosene lamps, for Bertie Connell's electricity served only public spaces. For years, the pervasive smell of burning kerosene from household lamps and the post office heater stayed with us. But change came. Although noisy, our thirty-two-volt generator provided lighting in our second house until SEC power connection occurred in 1955. It had its downside. The source of this earlier electric power was surrounded by choking exhaust fumes and rows of batteries in a shed at the end of our long backyard. When lights flickered and engine faltered, we scrambled to locate candles and lamps. Dad would abandon his meal – it always seemed to happen at mealtimes – don overalls and return with grease-coated hands. Strangely, he seemed not to resent the intrusion beyond uttering a 'Blast!' – his only expletive.

Our second house along the street was of unknown heritage. It required changes to the mainly male workplace (post office) and the kitchen where, apart from breakfast, Dad never assumed control. He and local, Bob Anderson, did the carpentry for both kitchen and post office. While the greater space of the new house excited us most, I found Dad's carpentry impressive because, in my Monday morning woodwork classes, sawing in a straight line presented me with an impossible challenge.

Few houses in the town were either more palatial or inferior to ours. An absence of such disparities further reinforced the feeling of our not being deprived, no matter how basic were our living conditions. It made me wonder whether shared poverty contributes less to human displeasure than big differences in material well-being. To some degree, the relatively low level of inequality in Walpeup and, by international standards, across Australia reinforced the myth that ours was the land of the fair go, the land of opportunity. Not that these concepts meant much to me then.

Louvre windows were popular. They comprised multiple panes opened or shut with a side lever. We had them installed in both post office and kitchen of our second house. They provided a conveniently adjustable opening through which Mum could keep tabs on people walking along the main street. In a sense, unlike Dad, she was a spectator rather than participant in the community. Standing by the sink, and looking through these louvres, we sometimes joined her and watched farmers, arms moving clockwork fashion, shrouded in veils of dust like Indonesian shadow puppets, pitching Mallee stumps with an echoing boom into open steel railway trucks. I was not privy to his inner thoughts, but I could imagine Dad thinking, thank God those days are gone.

Our newly constructed post office stood above an old cellar filled in with sand. It provided an ideal place to practise high jump. Although I understood little of gravity, I knew its effects. In high jump, I needed all the help I could get. With as much hope as enthusiasm, I was determined to perfect the western roll. Going over the bar horizontally to me was an improvement on the scissors method, when the body was vertical. That was the theory anyway.

The office was raised slightly above street level and had at its entrance two concrete steps where Dad and I sat to chat in the cool of a summer's evening.

Occasionally, Les Simpson would appear around the corner. Habitually, he paused, his head turning to the side like a magpie eyeing a worm. 'I don't think we'll be getting any rain' – an undoubtedly safe observation or similar overture – then would come the redundant 'Mind if I join you?'

In front of us, over beyond the plantation, beyond the goods shed, the station and the tennis courts, stretched miles of stunted Mallee scrub broken by a number of wheat and sheep farms linked by winding sandy tracks. One summer evening, we watched the night sky reddened by a lingering bushfire on the horizon out in Sunset country to the north. Our concern then was always for human safety, ignorant as we were of the fact that it might take a hundred years for Mallee ecology to be restored after fire. Mostly, casual chatting on the steps, no matter how shallow, was better than silence, and I valued yet another chance to enjoy the company of adults.

Dad made good use of the louvre window on the front wall of the post office. Undeterred by two decades of miserable toil on the farm, he was happy to chat at length with local farmer Bernie Lander. Most of their conversation centred on the Victorian Wheat and Wool Growers' Association, of which Bernie was an active member. From the snippets of conversation I overheard, Bernie's farm seemed to run itself.

Townspeople and farmers had access to external letter boxes beneath this same window and to the right. Not that many made use of them. They preferred to come inside, ostensibly to ask for mail but, in reality, just for a chat. To those who sought to be given mail after hours, Mum extended a frosty reception.

Inside, along one wall of the office, a number of pigeonholes enabled sorting of mail for outward distribution. Attached names complemented those I heard in the Saturday night's country football scores to form a sort of informal geography lesson. To their left, towards the war's end was a table often covered with parcels. Mostly circular, they were tins, fruit cake inside, sewn up in cotton cloth or hessian with addressee written in indelible pencil as part of a Food for Britain campaign. I was unaware whether the many families with German names contributed equally to this humanitarian cause. The full extent of bomb damage across England and Scotland was not well known, but with the death of Dad's brother, wife and son, we knew about the Blitz.

Opposite the table was the long main counter on which Dad leaned to chat and transact business with customers. Upright, at the house end of the office, stood a switchboard – what one might say was the nerve centre. Holes in rows, plugs inserted, when things were busy, they criss-crossed the board in a tangle like spaghetti. This was people's contact with the outside world, invisible messages flying hither and yon like bees in search of honey.

Mum, Dad and Fay shared the role of manning the switchboard, nominally with continuous service, but calls later than ten p.m. were a rare emergency. My older brother Bruce had left home at sixteen in 1952 when I was thirteen, and I was now an only child. The fact that I escaped doing my share of switchboard operating was a consequence of my being the youngest of five rather than any belief my schooling should not be interrupted. By this stage, few signs had emerged of this youngest son becoming a Rhodes Scholar.

More than merely a convenient facility for gossip, the party line was a precursor to modern mobile technology, the sort so important in the event of catastrophic fires like that of Black Saturday, 7 February 2009. On an infinitely smaller scale, in 1954, a blaze broke out on Zable's farm. Immediately it engaged Dad as postmaster and captain of the Walpeup Fire Brigade. Having sent urgent messages along the party lines, he attached a furphy tank – the town's fire truck – to the back of our car. I helped Dad load up knapsacks and beaters and we headed south to the scene. The Zable son, David, had been holding a magnifying glass above dry grass in near 100-degree temperatures to see what would happen. He soon found out. The blaze crackled at unstoppable speed towards a haystack and engulfed it. Our neighbour Digger's pumping the furphy was a futile as tackling a bushfire with a syringe. In short time, flames soared twenty metres high then quickly died to smouldering black remnants, watched by those wondering how it started. By now, young David had retreated indoors. For farmers, it was also a brief break from solitary work in the paddocks. Within a week, they rallied and another haystack appeared on the property. Next time it could be them.

Fruits of a Good Life

In the 1940s we lived close to the elements. Like creatures lower down the evolutionary scale, we were not above seeking out cool spots at the height of summer. Occasionally, my sister Fay, nine years my senior, made a bowl of a fluffy, lemon-flavoured dessert called Moonshine. She knew I liked the stuff, and it was a measure of her generous nature that I took for granted. She'd put it in the cool air beneath our 2,000-gallon rainwater tank, the source of water for drinking and washing clothes. The tank had other uses. In such an arid climate, fresh water was a precious item. There was little open water in the Mallee in which mosquitoes could breed. To kill the mossie larvae (wrigglers) that threatened to transform into adult insects, Dad poured a small dose of kerosene into the tank. Less dense than water, it provided a suffocating surface film without affecting the quality of what we drank.

While the interior of our house was small, land was not at a premium in Walpeup and so we, like our neighbours, had a big backyard. On one side, near an aged paling fence, held together by a flourishing of morning glory with its blue trumpet flowers, stood our outdoor dunny or toilet. Inside the familiar sloped-roof weatherboard structure, torn squares of the *Sun News Pictorial* threaded on string served as toilet paper. This early form of recycling made for frustrating reading. Thrones of contemplation like our toilet had their hazards. Deadly redback spiders had an aversion to bright lights, and with a front door attached for modesty's sake, a dunny's interior was assured of almost permanent darkness. It meant a little circumspection was prudent before lowering the necessary garment and mounting the throne.

The second hazard was that one's silent reverie could be rudely interrupted by a loud rattle, a gust of fresh air around the lower parts,

The author and Bruce at cricket, 1947.

a surge of creosote smell, then a loud scraping as the all too important can beneath was replaced. If I was quick, I could get the job done, pull up pants and race out to witness the dunnyman lugging the big black can on his shoulder out the back gate. He would sit it on the back of a truck alongside other cans lined up, some empty, others filled with grateful contributions from neighbours. A favourite joke circulated among kids. Q: What has forty cylinders and flies? A: The night cart. Except that at that time, it came by day. It was not as if other town or farm residents had nice shiny porcelain toilets. With everyone in the same boat, any small discomforts were accepted as penalties of living. And who was to complain if relief was at hand, if after a short walk?

On the other side of the yard, Dad established a fruit and vegetable garden – never flowers. It might have been a bloke thing or it might have reflected his past. Life on the farm from the early twenties until we abandoned it in 1942 had been one long grind, with little time for aesthetic considerations. This sense that all land had to be used productively probably shaped his thinking about the garden. The ephemeral nature of flowers might also have led to his desire to put effort into something more enduring. For all these reasons, his preference was for vegetables and fruit trees.

He must have begun planting the latter not long after moving in 1942, because they had passed gestation period and were bearing by the time I was old enough to engage in silent plundering. The fact that fruit was usually attached to vegetables as the route to good health was more than enough justification for my marauding behaviour. A nectarine tree crossed with a white peach yielded enough juicy sweet fruit to make us fructose addicts for life. I was presented with a dilemma. By taking the first pickings inside and offering them to others, I had to trade off the glow of magnanimity with the worry that I might miss out. As a result, ripe fruit didn't always make it to the house.

Dad waxed lyrical about persimmons and feijoas. The unusual rich orange colour of persimmons and their sweetness captivated me, but the way it seemed to suck on the mouth if picked too early was a lesson in patience. It was something I found hard to learn. What inspired Dad's interest in the exotic, uncommon species? His wartime experience? He had been a farmer for over twenty years and had toiled mightily to render sandy and limestone soils productive. Now, with slightly better soils, an assured water supply and a ready supply of cow manure from our own cow, he must have been inspired to try again. Very early, I could see the benign cycle of growing lucerne (alfalfa) and feeding it to the cow, which produced more dung, which we shovelled onto the garden to grow more tomatoes, beans, peas and sweetcorn – and lucerne.

It was not until my senior school years that I began milking our cow, the first a Jersey, then Molly, a big Friesian. Pulling down on the teats in a stripping motion, as many start off doing, seemed a bit unkind so I was glad to progress to the orthodox squeeze and gentle tug methods. If my concentration lapsed or I had forgotten to trim my fingernails, Molly wasn't averse to expressing her displeasure with a vigorous lashing of her tail. Only once did she kick the bucket and threaten to waste all my hard work. Sadly, while out grazing, she broke her leg and we had to call the butcher to collect her. I confess to no deep relationship with Molly but absented myself on the day of her transport to the snorty yards.

Seeing that I was the main human consumer, I could hardly

complain about the addition of milking to my chores. I always liked feeding the poddy calf. Its frisky-tailed eagerness delighted me, and I enjoyed its taut hard body pushing against me. I gave no thought that its mother might not be happy to be consigned to a life of perpetual pregnancy and separated from its offspring to satisfy our need for milk. To start the excited tail-wagger drinking, Mum taught me to put its bony and muscular head in the bucket of milk, something that took much of my strength. Then with my hand under the surface, I inserted a finger into its mouth to cause it to suck and thus take in milk. I pity a cow with its young drawing sustenance on its teats, because to me, it was like having my fingers filleted. We did supplement the calf's intake with bran and pollard but we never told it that we were offering skimmed milk stripped of its cream in the separator. Were we looking for excuses for this deceit? These calves after all had a short hold on life before they also headed for the snorty yards.

At one stage, we obtained several goldfish from Red Cliffs to put into the metre-high galvanised-iron tank of drinking water for the cow. Whether they were taken by an opportunistic bird, died of boredom from swimming endlessly around in circles, or choked in the gradual accumulation of cow saliva, I don't know, but these tiny red fish weren't with us for long.

Metaphorically, cream meant something refined or superior and it had a special place on Mallee tables. On bottled fruit for dessert or whipped into more solid state with added sugar, it filled those mystery bags called cream puffs, the favourite for gatherings or fund-raising stalls of country women. Many of them were members of the Country Women's Association (CWA). Although often a luxury, cream never flavoured coffee American-style because, for some time, the only drink with any pretensions to being coffee was sold as coffee and chicory. Chicory came from a plant roasted in kilns on Phillip Island. To spruce up its image, it was sold in tall bottles with a man wearing a fez on the label. Chicory was a native of Europe, but Turkey or Morocco were perhaps thought to be more exotic than Phillip Island.

Turning the handle of a cream separator was one of those things I did while dreaming about new places to trap rabbits or to find dead wool to collect and sell. I never quite worked out its function, but the separator had a floating disc in it that, when tapped in the sink during washing, would give out a resonant pluuuuunng, like long vibrations of an Indian sitar. Apart from its provocation to dream, this diversion was one of the few bonuses of using the separator and was as close as I ever got to a musical instrument.

The penultimate stage in the dairy processing was turning the handle of a wooden butter churn. It did not take long after a period of sloshing and slapping inside the churn for a solid to separate from buttermilk. I subcontracted to Mum the task of fashioning the butter into blocks with thin wooden pats, never knowing the purpose of ridges on the pats. Waste was never countenanced. Mum mixed residual buttermilk with flour to produce scones.

In Walpeup, much energy was expended in the name of survival. Besides milking, separating and making butter, it included gardening, turning a clothes wringer, lifting the handle of a washing machine to suck dirt out of clothes with a loud slurrrp, and other domestic chores like cleaning the bath with kerosene, cleaning the chook house, chopping Mallee stumps, gathering pine logs for the copper, splitting kindling or morning wood to set the fire going at day's break, even operating the pump handle for the town fire engine. In addition, we walked, often ran, and rode a bike everywhere. As a result of all this physical exertion, we never sat down to eat without feeling hungry nor felt any need to follow the advice of dieting specialists.

One enduring childhood activity that took little of my energy but gave continuous reward was raising chooks – chickens were always the juvenile form. Dad constructed most of their enclosure with me merely as assistant. Intuitively, in guiding my labours, he knew that the best form of instruction was to enjoy such shared activity and, like our forebears, to teach by example, rarely with explicit instruction.

I feel grateful for some of the pleasure chooks gave me during my errant thoughts in church. I sat there, glad that someone recommended Rhode Island Reds. They were bigger than White Leghorns, the most common breed of poultry around and my RIRs laid big eggs, much bigger than those that pass today as supermarket large eggs. I loved eating them but never considered that this behaviour put me on a par with marauding goannas, lizards, foxes and hawks for whom eggs are a prized food. Like most creatures in their infancy, the chickens' cuteness helped their survival. As day-olds they arrived by train in a cardboard box, like tiny, fluffy yellow ping-pong balls on stilts. I couldn't resist removing the box lid as, cheeping and jostling, they nuzzled up to the heated brick we wrapped in old flannel underwear out in the washhouse. They carried their appeal into adulthood. There is something calming about observing chooks clucking around looking for grain or seed, similar to the mesmerising effect of watching goldfish in a glass tank. It occurred to me that if Labrador dogs are favoured with an agreeable nature, then maybe different breeds of poultry also have different temperaments. My Rhode Island Reds were nothing if not companionable. When I squatted on my haunches, they needed no encouragement to flap up and land on my shoulder, chortling contentedly in my ear, little realising that one of their number would soon grace a dinner table. About this, I felt not a jot of guilt.

Local cultural norms and our conscience-driven mother meant that completion of chores and physical activity in general – cleaning the bath with kerosene, for example – took precedence over reading. Sport was fine, especially tennis. Closer settlement in Walpeup during the 1940s and 1950s meant plenty of use was made of the town's three gypsum tennis courts. Every Sunday, names chalked on a board ensured some sort of transparency and democratic access. In summer, Bruce and I played one game of tennis followed by another, except when duty called and we had to help to bottle fruit.

Nothing better fostered an ethos of self-sufficiency than Vacola preserving kits. *The Weekly Times*, that trusted broadsheet of rural Victoria with the pink cover (no suggestion of Communist associations!), carried advertisements for Vacola equipment. Keenly fought competition at the Royal Show guaranteed their widespread use. With her two young sons, Mum had a workforce – not always willing – to stone, peel and stuff case upon case of apricots, plums and peaches in the jars. In one summer we clocked up twelve cases. Each one weighing forty pounds (eighteen kilograms) arrived by steam train and later by its replacement, diesel railcar. Apricots were a snap: split them open, toss the seed away, stuff the halves in the jars, pour in syrup and fasten lids with a spring clip and there were your bottled fruit. As the name implies, clingstone peaches stubbornly resisted separation of fruit from seed. In the tussle, juice ran down our arms and justified savouring more than a few portions. Ripe clingstones were delicious. Finally, our job done, we put thermometer in the tubular space at the side of the pan now half-filled with water, which one of us heaved onto the stove. Mum's role was to ensure that the mercury column rose to the approved temperature and stayed there. I would like to think that our labours were leavened with lots of weighty discussions but in the absence of much serious reading by any of us, there was little encouragement for it.

Fruit preserved in this manner was our standard dessert. It would be preceded every day by lamb, usually as chops and often from something that was a lamb some time ago. Thus I learned the expression 'mutton dressed up as lamb' while oblivious of its usual sexist usage. We also enjoyed corned beef, and what is now considered indelicately as offal – kidneys, brains and lamb's fry – and a variety of fresh vegetables. While liver became lamb's fry and the stomach lining of sheep became tripe, kidney and brains needed no such euphemism. I'm sure that tripe survived as a dish only because of the ingredients served with it, much like the stone soup of children's fables. Mostly, vegetables came from our own garden but they were supplemented by some from farmers whose bread we delivered gratis. Our trees gave us nectarines, apricots and quinces in abundance. The fact that they ripened gradually meant our Vacola labours were tied to fruit importation. It took some time before I could enjoy the sweetness of pumpkin and cabbage, in part because Mum believed that they had to be thoroughly sterilised before serving. Corned beef (silverside) I never tired of. I liked its saltiness. Routinely, for my school lunch, Mum prepared lamb and tomato sandwiches. Their inevitable unappetising sogginess led me to start cutting my own sandwiches and experimenting with other novel fillings in our jaffle iron.

Oranges and apples for immediate eating also arrived by rail in forty-pound cases. Winter's nights we sat in the comforting warmth of Mallee stumps glowing in the open fireplace steadily going through our supply of oranges. Although white stumps burnt more quickly than red, they filled gaps in conversation with their pyrotechnics: gas spitting out in jets of blue, red and orange flames. Sometimes, it was enough just to watch the flames and let thoughts take over, an inland substitute for endless breaking of waves on the seashore. When we had no more plans to make, reminiscences or grumbles to air, when tiredness took over and the fire was almost extinguished with orange peel, we retreated to bed in unheated bedroom and sleepout.

Understandably, in a community of few people, many of them out on farms and only converging on the town on a Saturday or for a special event, the unplanned always caused great excitement. While not exactly a loaves and fishes occasion, the good Lord demonstrated his beneficence in the form of apples, a whole semi-trailer load of them. It happened right at the end of town where the road took a sharp and steeply cambered turn right before it straightened up to head to Ouyen. The driver, mindful of the sloping road – steeper than the side of a velodrome – sought to avoid tipping over inwards when negotiating the curve at too slow a speed. He therefore opted to ride the upper edge, but he over-compensated. Speed thrust the vehicle outward, it toppled over, spraying shattered cases of Jonathans and dozens of smashed and intact bottles of beer in a chaotic mess over a wide area. Within sight of the carnage, I grabbed a sugar bag and was one of the first on site, salivating at the prospect of unlimited crisp, juicy apples. News of the mishap swept the town. Telephone party lines swung into action and residents raced through the plantation and down to the railway crossing. Gingerly they stepped through the mass of broken bottles, in some cases guiltily, others with abandon, filling as many bags with apples as they could carry. My mind full of Jonathans, I filled half a sugar bag, all I could carry with any dignity. Some, no doubt the more God-fearing Christians, must have wondered whether taking advantage of another's misfortune was the most moral thing to do. Nevertheless, the beer went early.

Voyage Around My Mother

Mum was not zealous in her efforts to produce God-fearing children. But she left her stamp on all the family in other ways, most regrettably on Fay. Throughout her life, my sister carried the deeply incised wounds of relentless maternal discrimination. Mum was never remotely an evil person. She just embodied the unconscious sexism of her era and, were it not for my combative nature (an attribute, paradoxically, I inherited in no small part from her), I would have been an even greater beneficiary of such gender bias.

In the early 1980s as we drove to Mum's funeral, Fay said to me, 'You know that you were Mum's favourite.'

'You must have had it tough then,' I said, a little ashamed I knew little of how my sister was treated.

Everyone has a back story. The second youngest of ten children, Mum inherited some of the frugal ways of her Scottish mother. The spectre of unrelieved hardship on the farm during the Depression must have reinforced these tendencies. A probable consequence was that she endorsed my various money-making ventures, and it was something I took for granted. Dying at the age of eighty-three, she spent most of her life in small southern Mallee towns and largely pre-technological at that. Television – and a host of other diversions and comforts – did not arrive in Australia until 1956, the year before my parents moved to Melbourne.

Like many of her generation, she was driven by duty to her children, in whom she imbued the virtue of busyness. If given the choice, her children would have preferred a bit of overt affection. If she did not say, 'The devil lurks in idle hands', it did seem as if she had taken out a life subscription to the Protestant work ethic. To what extent

Mother, age 69, 1968.

this attitude was related to the feeling that her own work was never done, I don't know. Having unfinished tasks can also bring a sense of purpose and in a sexist era, self-assertion probably took many forms. Such was her battle against idleness that we were left with the sense that work was never finished and reading was a sin. Unlike my father, she did not read books nor, to any extent, the *Sun News Pictorial*, even though numerous photos took up much of its space. I also can't recall its contents being the topic of stimulating or extended conversation in our household.

While Mum seemed to display a small range of emotional and intellectual resources to handle what was put upon her, objectively, she had endured conditions on the farm that would have withered the hardiest of plants. Had I known this in my youth, I might perhaps have been more tolerant of her ways. A contributing factor to Mum's disgruntlement was that she seemed not to be able to pass off the jibes of a mother-in-law whom she hated intensely. It consumed her. It was not helped by the fact that, according to her, Dad did not defend her in front of his mother. I saw none of this; Dad's parents died before my birth.

One aspect of my interaction with her cannot be overlooked. It is also not something I'm proud of. In the absence of the socialising benefits of peer group, magazines, talkback radio and television, I relied heavily on my mother to help me negotiate the slights and challenges of adolescence. I offloaded too much on someone who was ill-equipped through her own limited experience and, sometimes, by her volatile displays. Unquestionably driven by wanting to do her best for me, she tried, and unquestionably, I heaped excessive demands on her. My own lack of maturity meant I was unable to see what I was doing or appreciate Mum's efforts.

Everyone can recall childhood incidents that seem indicative or symbolic of something more enduring. If grievance is embedded in it, the memory can be especially sharp. Although trips to the Red Cliffs dentist did address most of our problems, we did have toothache. For me, the cloves treatment did not seem to work. I sat on my bed, my back to the sleepout wall, complaining and, in a rare display of physical affection, Mum took her place beside me to offer comfort. The pain of her sitting on my arm took over from the toothache and I gave voice. She bounded off, muttering disgust at my ingratitude and left me to my toothache. At my young age, I had not learned tact or subtlety but, arguably, there were alternatives available to my mother too. But what remains is the sense that it highlighted her inability to offer physical closeness. Two consequences probably follow from the incident. First, given that we learn by modelling and experience, in their absence, touching has to be a calculated rather than spontaneous act. Second, if the only time that affection comes is in the presence of pain or illness, then there is an incentive to highlight them to secure the affection. And it is a habit difficult to kick through life.

Mum never left the house without a hat, partly because it was fashion for both men and women, but also to protect an unblemished porcelain complexion that she carried to her death. People often spoke of it with admiration and sometimes a little envy. Tidily, if not expensively dressed, when visiting, attending a funeral or Anzac Day, she walked upright, handbag always under her arm. It was not for boys to comment on such matters but secretly, I respected this aspect of my mother.

While offering little encouragement for her children to read – in fact, she made clear that it had to take second place to chores – Mum drew scant satisfaction from some of the activities in which she did engage. There was one thing she seemed to bear with shame: her large and strong hands. Genetic inheritance aside, it could well have reflected the continuing physical nature of her existence – the ringing of sheets in the Monday wash, for example. Did she unconsciously equate her hands to those of a peasant woman? Or just an early form of body dysmorphia? During her determined knitting endeavours – notably for us and not herself – Bruce and I would ask her, 'Which Christmas were you planning those socks for, Mum?' One of her triumphs was a tight fitting polo-necked green jumper she made for me when I was sixteen years old and, nearly seventeen, I wore in my first year of university. It spelt out in capital letters my country hick origins to all the suave students from Melbourne's prominent families sauntering in their ski tans up the library aisle.

Mum managed only six years of primary schooling, she said, because her family moved out of horse-riding distance. Possibly when it came time to discipline me, her days on horseback came to mind. With little skill in reading the signs, I once again pushed her to the limit and she descended on me with lip-curling rage, brandishing a riding whip. There was nothing so terrifying as Mother out of control. Still young enough at around eight to be immobilised with terror, I saw no escape. In her hand was a forty-centimetre-long and tapering leather-encased device that might have spurred a horse to greater heights but when laid strongly about my legs produced biting pain followed by impressive red welts. Not long after, I vengefully chopped the thing into pieces and buried it in the ashes bin destined for the town tip. There was never further mention of this missing weapon of maternal warfare.

A variety of circumstances conspired to deny women of my mother's generation the opportunities many of them desired. With Mum, it was epitomised in her frequent wish to have been able to play more tennis. To her, life was about work. Custom dictated that Monday was washing day. The ritual was even deserving of a dedicated washhouse attached to the back of the house. In pride of place, a large copper recessed in brick with ample space for Murray pine logs to be burnt for fuel underneath. As if each week they had to be disinfected of some contagious disease, sheets were pushed under boiling water with a piece of wood of thick broom handle dimensions, furry at the end from years of ritual prodding. Not only did it have to be strong enough to lift a sheet dripping with steaming water, but so did Mum's back. Held aloft momentarily to drain a little, she fed it into one of two stone troughs filled with best tank water. Now able to be lifted by hand, and directed through a hand-operated wringer, it was plunged into the adjoining trough of cold water, sky-blue from a dissolved block of Reckitt's Blue. To me, its only role seemed to be aesthetic. More wringing and into a cane washing basket ready to be hauled out to the clothes line strung across the backyard. In summer sun, washing flapping on the clothes line was crispy dry before the last basket was pegged out.

In all the laundry labours, no music. Even the Volga Boatmen could have provided a distracting chorus and it might have made lifting dripping sheets seem lighter. One very practical thing she made – because it saved bending – was a canvas peg bag she wore suspended in front and strapped around her waist. I knew enough about the arduous, boring nature of these Monday activities from my occasional and mostly insignificant involvement during school holidays.

My childhood in the forties and early fifties was hardly a time of bewildering technological change. In nowhere was this more evident than in the washhouse. One of our earlier possessions was a washing machine. It had the capacity to magnify the output of human effort equivalent to that of pumping our Furphy fire tank to fight a haystack fire. Our washing machine consisted of a large cone bigger than a Vietnamese rural hat attached to a handle spanning a sturdy drum. When the handle was lifted up and down the cone created a suction in the water, a noise reminiscent of the little boys' farts that seemed to bring endless delight and sometimes admiration. Its mission was to punish clothes for being dirty. Using it was still about manpower or, more strictly, womanpower. A big advance came with the purchase of an electrically driven Simpson washing machine. In nice green enamel, it had a central shaft with a couple of wings that swished the water back and forth with determined efficiency. I could see Mum's relief that it saved some work but there was still the wringer.

Before the advent of Velvet soap for washing hands, body and clothes on Mondays, Mum made soap, big blocks of it. She heated lard from butcher or farm in the washhouse copper with caustic soda until it solidified into a creamy brown substance later cut into big blocks. While it while it got an E grade for lather, we were never short of it.

Although we bought bread, we must have used enough McAlpine's flour in cotton bags to provide an ample supply of handkerchiefs (or hankies) that Mum ran up on the sewing machine. I was never self-conscious about our hankies. They seemed to do the job. When not cutting up flour bags for hankies, she was darning our socks on a mushroom-shaped wooden device. All of this conservation activity was more a legacy of the Great Depression and a non-consumerist Protestant ethic embodied in the adage, waste not, want not, than any conscious act of recycling.

In many poorer communities, maternal care for children seems to be expressed in provision of food. For us, it was basically regarded as a fuel, the prerequisite to continuous activity and sound health. Haute cuisine was indeed a foreign concept. I was therefore more than happy to accept a departure from functional cooking when Mum made a frequent and very welcome batch of Anzac biscuits from oatmeal and golden syrup. These she stored in a cylindrical tin identical to one used as a container for her stockings. Making an after-school beeline from bus to kitchen for the Anzacs sometimes led to disappointment.

Mum was also sufficiently adept at sponge-making to provide the base ingredient for lamingtons. For this widely popular luxury food, sponge was cut into rectangular blocks, dipped in melted chocolate and coated in desiccated coconut. The other main use for home-made sponge, combined with jelly and preserved peaches, was in wine trifle. A non-drinker, Mum routinely tilted the port wine bottle, uttering a predictable 'Oops!' as the deep red liquid gurgled over the chunks of sponge. No one objected, but we could never persuade her to take her fruit cakes out of the oven earlier. By comparison with those of city-dwelling Aunt Jean, whose efforts were delightfully soggy, Mum's fruit cakes tended towards dryness.

Part of the then parental role was to fill in any perceived health-threatening gap in our diet. Thank goodness we were never obliged to take the creamy medical supplement Hypol. Its smell was an immediate provocation to retching as I discovered when I removed the lid of a discarded bottle. To be fair, the use-by concept wasn't common and Hypol might not have contained preservative. Centuries ago, blood-letting was the guarantor of good health. Mum's focus was on strengthening and preserving what blood we had. Therefore, one of our health supplements was lots of minced red meat, fortunately cooked in shepherd's pie. Sulphur and treacle we consumed for similar purpose. An occasional dose of cod liver oil, to move the bowels, we gulped down as quickly as possible. We had no recourse to a chemist and luckily for us, there was none, if their role was to dispense Hypol and cod liver oil.

In what was largely Mum's domain, the washhouse, we also stored an occasional side of pork, well-salted for morning bacon. Since we had no pigs, it was a gift from a grateful farmer along the mail run. It often figured alongside Dad's breakfast favourite, sour tomatoes, whose other ingredients were vinegar and a little sugar, all cooked in a frying pan. Whether it was produced with Dad's enthusiastic endorsement, or simply that he was the cook, I probably gave it greater approval than was strictly justified. Mum carried the overwhelming burden in the kitchen but in the best tradition of aspiring chefs, Dad never disparaged his own efforts. In what must have been a preference for one of the taste categories, another of his favourites was sour eggs – uncooked but beaten with vinegar. In short, that was Dad's culinary repertoire. Since the journey from chook to breakfast table was always short, we never encountered salmonella from raw egg. Otherwise, for breakfast, oatmeal porridge, very slightly salted, served with sugar and milk was a staple. Very occasionally we had bought cereal. The cover of the Weetie packet represented a brilliant marketing device for even the faintly curious youngster. It showed progressively smaller images of Mr Weetie holding a Weetie packet showing Mr Weetie holding a Weetie packet and so on – a glimpse into infinity. Food for both mind and stomach.

As young children, we dutifully lined up for a series of preventive injections. But mumps and chickenpox slipped in under the radar, not that we were alone in the neighbourhood in succumbing. Measles were much talked about but probably not more than that. Somewhere around my entry into secondary school, Bruce and I went down – literally because we hadn't the energy to walk – to a most unusual sickness that kept us bedridden for two weeks. So weakened were we that I hadn't the strength to lift the new second-hand bike our parents bought. The diagnosis was viral encephalitis, believed to have been transported by mosquitoes. In 1950, rumours circulated that humans could also acquire myxomatosis from the vector mosquitoes. Then as now, it was not enough for the dispassionate findings of science to convince people; extreme steps had to be taken to gain public acceptance. It took the courage of virologists Fenner, Macfarlane Burnett and Clunies Ross, who injected themselves with the myxoma virus, to prove that what was devastating for rabbits would not harm humans.

Just as routine as the childhood injections was an operation to remove tonsils. They had to be wrenched out whether they were a problem or not. A tonsillectomy was a sort of rite of passage. Olfactory memories can be powerful. I will never forget the smell of chloroform and the nausea as I grabbed the bars of the hospital bed in a writhing struggle to regain consciousness. When I did, Mum felt that her nine-year-old would benefit from some vitamin C. The orange juice I gulped down was the closest approximation to sulphuric acid I could imagine but something I never felt inclined to put to the test.

Mum's life illustrated the fact that opportunity blocked was also potential denied. Certainly, there were signs that she found her circumstances frustrating. Her experience from the time of their marriage in the early 1920s to when, in 1942, our family left the farm, would have challenged even the most resourceful. It was a period that also included the Great Depression.

One value that she helped to instil was deferred gratification, a necessity when the chances for immediate gratification were few. And it came in handy. Given the nature of our schooling, there had to be a fair bit of such deferral to stay in the system. Even though – or because – Mum had a short six years of schooling, it did not shake her belief in its value. It is strange that she did not bemoan her lack of education except that she seemed to want me to 'make something' of myself. Dad had an additional two years to complete his merit certificate, or Grade 8, the expected limit for most early in the twentieth century. Both supported my continuing education. Far from being helicopter parents, they provided no pressure to succeed and, if I didn't, would assure me that 'You can only do your best.' One trait they did encourage was persistence, and in later years, this showed in my determination to succeed in the face of negative evaluations. My perseverance was also possibly an attempt to achieve maternal approval in a manner I could control when there were few overt displays of affection. Still, it is undeniable that she did her best.

We ate well at home and apart from viral complaints that kids seemed to get, we kept good health, assisted by abundant exercise. We did little to boost Mrs Dickie's sales of soft drink and dried-out lollies, yet tooth decay was endemic. We all suffered from the lack of a fluoridated water supply, and so an enterprising dentist never wanted for custom.

Did the dentist have a surgery somewhere? Perhaps he only had an itinerant existence, but in my early childhood, every Saturday morning a dentist would station his caravan in front of the Walpeup coffee palace. I don't recall any electric cables to drive the drill. To imagine a pedal-operated one is not fanciful, but maybe our friendly dentist did do some repair work even if the evidence was that he did very little. On his departure, there was always a small pyramid of decayed teeth on the roadside. Evidently, the spittoon had no bottom to it. Pubescent girls and boys alike lost their teeth indiscriminately, even their front ones. The consequences for their self-esteem are too awful to contemplate.

Mum felt we were deserving of something better. Our need was great because all three siblings at home were dealt a poor hand when it came to dental health despite constant assaults on bacteria with elbow-bending brushing. My excessive vigour in teeth cleaning was a response to older brother Ian, who did everything with gusto.

His language was significant. 'Don't forget to scrub your molars!'

I knew that the reminder also included incisors. I also learnt later, when gums receded, that gentle brushing rather than scrubbing was needed.

No dentist plied his trade in Ouyen and the one in Red Cliffs, a long drive on gravel road, was the nearest. Perhaps because of the distance, our dental visits left nothing to chance. In one day, my sister Fay had numerous injections and six fillings. I can still hear the squeak of dobs of amalgam being pressed into what remained of my teeth. This industrious excavation and filling began when I was young, such that by my mid-teens, my fillings had moved into their second edition.

Our dentist did all the right things – white coat, antiseptic surgery – but his reassuring efforts left me unconvinced. And there was his breath. Or did it come from an uncooperative stomach? It was a veritable banquet of foul bacteria. In retrospect, it should have been a professional handicap. But Mum stuck with him because he was well-meaning, and way back he had somehow guaranteed my grandparents' continuing ability to eat solid food.

Aware that even going to school might have been preferable to visiting the dentist, my mother took us to a Red Cliffs restaurant for a luncheon treat.

The immaculately suited restaurateur, silver hair, red flower in buttonhole, motioned us with a forced smile to a table covered in lace table cloth. He took great care not to obscure a photo of an attractive young woman prominently displayed on his desk. 'My daughter,' he said with evident pride. 'She was a model, you know. Now she's married to the president of Lebanon.'

Or was she just dating him and he had high hopes for his daughter?

Despite the proprietor's new-found Middle Eastern connection, the meal was distinctly Australian: vegetables reduced to mush and lamb peaks emerging from a sea of gravy. Not that the quality of food was my main concern. By this time, my jaw had locked from holding it open all morning and it was more than I could do to stop dribbling over my frozen lips into the gravy.

In that era, needles took on frightening harpoon dimensions and I had become used to the euphemistic 'Just a little prick.'

Our dentist's custom was to drive home the injection and then attend to my brother Bruce in an adjoining surgery while my anaesthetic staggered towards its paralysing objective. Periodically, he'd come back and give my gums a poke to assess the progress of face numbing. 'A bit longer,' he'd say, with the comforting satisfaction of a country woman testing a cake with a skewer.

Meanwhile, my infantile thoughts fluctuated between guilt and wistful memories of the small doses of chocolate that had quietly supplemented the destructive work of genes. The business of numbing didn't stop at nerves and gums. It affected everything below my eyes. Our dentist believed in carpet bombing.

Afternoon saw more of the same: More needles, more jackhammer pounding from the drill, more spitting, a grinding and sanding, and finally, release. Or so we thought. The long trip home in encroaching darkness was no treat. Car sickness meant we pulled over to punctuate the still, roadside air with our retching. With paralysed lips, even that had its problems. To our relief, these dental visits weren't frequent.

Aged Grandparents and Their Children

Besides a large backyard and its potential to continue gardening, our new residence further down Walpeup's main street had a back veranda. There for several years my ninety-plus grandmother, grey hair in bun, a Whistler-type figure, sat wrapped in a shawl and blanket in a cane chair, her big round glasses staring blankly over the back garden. She also appears in a late nineteenth-century sepia photo of four adult figures, standing rigidly – she, her mother and three siblings – in lace-trimmed black full-length black dresses and wearing forbiddingly severe expressions.

Originally, my great-grandmother and four very young children took the perilous ship voyage from Scotland in the late 1850s, when the gold rushes were still in full swing. Nevertheless, my childhood imagination did not stretch to the hardships they must have endured on their long sea voyage – not least, wretched sea-sickness. Grandma still retained her Scottish accent and in my brief but forgettable conversations with her, I realised that my obligation to be a respectful grandson came with a measure of boredom for me. But there was a legacy. The halo effect of family conversation was that I long retained the view that Scots were of superior stuff, and implicitly trustworthy. Such is the force of unconscious bias. Grandma died aged ninety-three.

In the early 1940s, prior to her coming to live with us, we drove 125 kilometres to Red Cliffs to have Christmas dinner with her and Grandpa in their humble cottage. A still functioning citrus orchard grew just metres from their back door and a breeze gently moving along the evergreen rows tempered the scorching dry air.

In the late 1880s, the Chaffey brothers from California saw the potential of this climate and envisioned a future for irrigated

Maternal grandparents, circa 1940.

horticulture alongside the Murray River. (Their story was told in *Water Into Gold* by Ernestine Hill, a copy of which I received as Dux of Ouyen high school and, to my shame, I've not yet read.) My grandparents must have been early adopters but, by this Christmas, my guess was that my grandfather was long past mounting ladders to pick oranges.

In their tiny cottage, space was at a premium. Cream and green woodwork showed signs of wear, the shelves were cluttered, and inspirational homilies hung on the wall. My grandfather, white hair, long white beard, shuffling towards his final year at ninety-six, hovered around like Father Time. A Carmichael, he must have had Scottish ancestry but his overwhelming presence was age.

A solitary visit like this fell short of enough to make personal connection with him and I could see that he was unlikely to be host many more times. Mum fussed about stuffing the turkey, topping beans, cutting up potatoes, pumpkin and carrots and checking the water level as the Christmas pudding bubbled away in its last two hours' cooking. No matter that temperatures nudged towards 100 degrees, a roast dinner was beyond question. Along with Christmas cards featuring snow-capped European pines, what we ate to celebrate Christmas said much about our still derivative culture.

Memorably, one Christmas dinner among the orchards started in unorthodox fashion. Next door, one of the old couple's ten children – and my uncle – had a fruit block and a son with twin passions. Sharing my brother Ian's hobby, he built balsa wood model aeroplanes that he hung from the garage ceiling. He armed himself with an airgun and like a bloke at a fairground shooting gallery impressing his girlfriend, he tried to hit mice running along the rail in their garage. With mouse shooting and balsa aircraft the likes of which we had also flown and assembled, the pre-dinner Christmas entertainment had more than passing appeal.

While I enjoyed turkey and all the trappings, for me they were mere preparation for the plum pudding to follow. The dish's ancestry goes back to mixtures of meat and vegetables Romans cooked to make their food last, but the current form of pudding dates from 1830s England. I loved the stuff and regretted it was only an annual event because, no matter how much I liked the taste, at the fifth helping taste became secondary. I was focused intently on silver coins liberally distributed throughout the pudding mixture. Any concerns about the use of suet (pig fat) as an ingredient had not yet surfaced. If I had been worried, it would have been readily dismissed. At dinner's end, I found the most comfortable position was to lie flat on the floor to provide maximum extension for my stomach, grateful that those present were all too old to engage in active games. By this time, I had expressed my profound appreciation for presents received and felt I could lie down undisturbed.

Our subsequent visits to Sunraysia – to Redcliffs – were for dental repair, to remove impediments to the pleasures of eating. Given that I never lacked a hearty appetite, anything that facilitated further eating, no matter how unpleasant, was worth enduring.

Even the humble Christmas pudding traditionally cooked in a cloth featured in a newspaper comic strip. The suet ingredient or its being wrapped in cloth gave the pudding a leathery outer skin.

Comic strip country hicks, Ben Bowyang and Bill Smith were mates.

Turning to whiskered Bill, Ben asked, 'Hey, Bill, I was wondrin' if I could have the cloth back from the Christmas pudding me wife made for yer.'

'Chripes, Ben, was there a cloth around it?'

I don't think I ever saw the comic strip but it appealed to my childish humour when Dad repeated it.

Mum was the second youngest of the ten children. By virtue of their age and their widespread distribution, many of the uncles and aunts were little more than names to me. Aunt Moyna in Melbourne was distinguished by her husky smoker's voice and capacity to laugh. In the absence of much mirth at the dinner table at home, I warmed to her. On her rare visits, Aunt Colina came with a stoop and a funereal demeanour. I thought she was Aunt Cleaner, an epithet that seemed fitting for one seemingly burdened by life. Her gloom was contagious so, having made my greeting, I would leave the two sisters to it. She had cause to be defeated. Her husband, Uncle Charlie, seemed to grow just enough wheat to justify his spending most of his time away on Victorian Wheat and Wool Growers Association business while she was forced to water a struggling garden by bucket out on the margins where good sense would say the country was too tough for plants or humans. Charlie possibly also felt that talking about grain and sheep policies with mates was more fun than steering horses around the field.

I formed a totally wrong impression of Auntie Jean, who owned or perhaps rented a two-storey inner-city house. On first meeting, she seemed to be another in the sad club. She had good reason. The one big love of her life had just been killed in a car accident. No wonder the atmosphere in her home on that occasion was grim. At others, her upright posture, big bosom and long string of pearls, mistakenly led me to think she was a wealthy dowager when in fact she ran a boarding house for three people. Never married, she treated me and siblings with singular thoughtfulness and affection, despite our different ages and temperaments. What joy she would have brought to any offspring! At around eight years old, when I had the good fortune to stay overnight at her place in Jolimont, she brought to me in bed a cup of tea and honeyed toast – what I then called 'supper before breakfast'. I felt special, but her distinctive ability was to convey to the younger three of us – brother, sister and me – the sense that we mattered. Earlier, although she had worked as a governess in a small private school, her support for my education in the public sector never wavered.

All three of Auntie Jean's boarders seemed to treat her with respect. Miss Walford, who worked as a secretary in the nearby CBD, was always pleasant if a little tense and vigilant. While I appreciated the questions she asked me, I had the impression that some of them were born of learned politeness and, without being secretive, she rationed her presence. Mr Boloton's life was bound up with live theatre, in which he was an accompanist. Fortunately for him, Melbourne had several venues staging vaudeville, pantomime, drama and mixed magic and gymnastics. Given these associations, his flair and flamboyance seemed appropriate, although Mallee life did little to foster sensitivity to differences of identity. Gap-toothed, grey-haired with wisps dangling, Miss Nubley could well have been a sibling to Mrs Surrerier, the one who spied on me over the fence as I assaulted her chickens playing havoc with our vegetable garden. No one could better cast two of Macbeth's three sisters. Despite Miss Nubley's distracting appearance, she embodied some of the assurance, the cultural capital of the sunken middle-class. She also shared some of Miss Walford's earnestness. With all three, I felt that I benefited second hand from the respect they showed my aunt.

Religion for the Non-believer

It was our turn to host the minister for Sunday dinner. The dearth of other takers, more than our sporadic church attendance, earned us the right to offer our hospitality. Leading the Presbyterian Church's charm offensive was the Reverend Mr Collard. Despite his sporting the obligatory collar, with his handsome looks he could have moonlighted for a Myer's catalogue. A good thing too, as I otherwise found God's delegates a little intimidating.

Despite our young reverend's attempt to put us at ease, I'd been warned in no uncertain terms that no beetroot must be spilled on the white table cloth. I even did my best to hide my surprise at the emergence of freshly ironed serviettes.

Best cold lamb, neatly sliced, fresh bread sliced to perfection, dressing applied and salad tossed, Mum, was, as ever, in charge. She said, 'Mr Collard will say grace.'

A brief moment of silence, a quizzical look, and 'Grace who, Mum?' followed by a swift and painful kick to my shin beneath the table.

With a disarming smile, our youthful minister ignored my indignant writhing and switched to asking whether my older brother Bruce and I had other siblings. I explained.

We had three. Two of them fled the nest soon after my birth. Ian, fifteen years my senior, fled the boring and hated farm life to become a World War II commando on Timor; Neta, more than a year older still, escaped to enter teachers' college. Neta therefore had virtually no presence in my childhood. Fay, nine years older than me, became relieving postmaster in various Mallee towns soon after completing her Year 10 (Intermediate Certificate), the final year of the then Ouyen Higher Elementary School. We waited impatiently for the treasured

Fay, age 17, 1947.

Violet Crumble, Cherry Ripe and at least two comics she brought home from her relieving duties. When not engaged away in such a responsible role, Fay also acted as surrogate mother to her two younger brothers because Mum doled out demonstrations of physical affection very economically. Before Sunday school or Anzac ceremonies, Fay ensured we were impeccably dressed: clean short pants suit, shiny shoes, socks firmly held high with garters, and finally, hair clean and brushed. Nevertheless, it prompted me to wonder where Fay learnt such caring behaviour.

In Walpeup, religion was not a social lubricant equal to sport – football, cricket, tennis or netball – and certainly alcohol. But architecturally, as a proportion of the thirty-two houses, churches had to be acknowledged as important. There were four – for the arithmetically minded, one church for every eight houses. Their location suggested an unspoken, contested hierarchy – a hierarchy only vocalised in chants of 'Catholic dogs sit on logs' among the young. Never morphing into overt hostility, the Catholic/Protestant division was more a matter of soft tribalism: talk behind closed doors and occasional social distance. The Catholic church graced the crest of Mount Walpeup: solid red brick with a gesture towards buttresses. Nineteenth-century Irishmen had laid claim to similar elevated real estate in other country towns. To some, preference for such sites was a desire to achieve the dominance that Australian society would not grant them. Nevertheless, many Catholic churches seemed more grandiose than the collections that could reasonably be squeezed from the pockets of poor Mallee farmers warranted. Once they emerged with their sins forgiven from this Walpeup Catholic house of worship, attendees received a double blessing from fine wind-borne spray wafting from leaking water towers opposite.

Lined up with its Irish competitor, but down the hill towards the town stood the Church of England. Cement sheet but nice green wooden trim.

The Methodists tucked their church modestly away in the scrub on the edge of town. It had a working-class humility, perhaps an echo of the church's English mining village origins. Service, not show, was its mission. It did, however, provide comfort for its parishioners in the form of an outdoor dunny in which, during the week, Lacey Clements and I coughed our way through a packet of Monopole Midget cigars to the evident discomfort of resident spiders.

I had inside knowledge of the Presbyterian Church, the galvanised-iron and wooden edifice sitting beside the road leading down to the town's water supply dam. Mum never told us why she hauled us off for irregular trips to its services. She might have been driven by intermittent pangs of conscience. My feelings about it were constant. I found it foreign, mostly meaningless, and the seats very hard.

As best I could gather, Mum took us to church because it was simply what she thought well-raised children did. On reflection, this adherence to norms of good behaviour was somewhat in conflict with the way she treated Walpeup residents. She was never good at making friends. Nevertheless, her own early Sunday school experience apparently scored some runs. She told me, 'The rainbow that rarely graced our skies was God's message about The Flood' (capital T and capital F). I think it was something about not having to face another one. I found this message reassuring, but the prospects of a great flood occurring in dry dusty Walpeup still seemed a tad remote.

Inside our church, the pulpit stood authoritatively above the hard, wooden benches lined up below. Its elevation told me that any words delivered from it were going to be very important. On our left, Mrs Graham, the volunteer organist, would insert the numbers of the day's hymns in their frame, much like petrol prices outside a Seven Eleven today. During the service, I deliberately stood beside Mr Walton, who had the loudest and most resonant voice. It was enough that organised religion seemed designed to highlight my insignificance without rubbing it in by expecting me to sing. The tiny congregation would not be outdone. When heavy rain occasionally pounded the galvanised-iron roof, parishioners rose to the challenge and sang louder.

The Reverend Collard's predecessor, Mr Vine, was born with only four fingers on his right hand, and rather pointy ones at that. I could not understand why he chose to raise that same hand for the benediction. Surely it was no great advertisement for God's beneficence, and contemplating the reverend's digit deficiency only distracted me more from his benediction. In truth, by this stage, my mind was usually on getting out of there.

During such irregular church attendance, I was preoccupied with squeezing water blisters on my hands, attempting to ignore my numb backside, and making sense of words like forgiveness, redemption and salvation. My thoughts were mostly elsewhere: wheelbarrowing cow manure for the garden – an activity possibly the cause of my water blisters – or stretching anti-raptor wire netting over our newly built henhouse.

Mum's uncertainty about the moral side of child-rearing meant she outsourced some of the responsibility to whatever religious agency was available. For example, at her instigation, Bruce and I found ourselves sitting in the supper room of the Memorial Hall on the way down the hill from primary school. With faltering interest, we watched an earnest husband and wife team of evangelists placing felt figures on a board to illustrate biblical stories. This arrangement, I could see, saved time and chalk. I found the stories a little implausible and struggled to see their relevance to my life – a continuing problem I had with formal religion. On this occasion, had the couple said to me, 'If you're planning to study English poetry later on, you'll find that the works of Blake, Gerard Manley Hopkins, T.S. Eliot and Milton are replete with biblical allusions,' I'd have been focused like a fighter pilot at a briefing session.

As a break from pinning felt figures, the evangelists insisted we join them to sing, 'Build your house upon the rock and not upon the sand', only cementing my view of religion's relevance to life in Walpeup. For a start, the only rock around was pebbles of limestone. In addition, any house building we might do was a long way off. But then I was a literalist from birth. The couple could sense my ambivalence, and I'm not sure whose interest waned first. It would have been interesting to know what the couple's dinner table conversation was like after their fruitless efforts, whether it shook their faith at all.

One of the most concentrated doses of religion-related activity was what I uncharitably called a Bible-bashers' camp in the forested hills on the fringes of Melbourne. This unflattering title did creep into family conversation – mainly from Dad – but perhaps not enough, as I was still seduced into attending by the word 'camp'. After all, fishing camps with my father on the Murray were utter bliss. I no doubt received encouragement from Mum to attend, but I have to own my part and add it to my list of life's bad decisions.

It was a disaster. I arrived late, after everyone already seemed to be best of friends. In the communal session, they clapped and chorused their way through songs of praise they knew word-perfect. Transported with the fervour of their faith, they all seemed SO HAPPY! That first night, even sleep did not relieve my misery. Sprawled in tents and sleeping on canvas stretchers, I felt the malicious cold rising up to penetrate every bit of skin and flesh, every muscle, every bone of my body. I twigged to the problem. The ground was soaking wet. I lay there, working on a strategy to get myself out of this mess. Mercifully, in the early hours of morning, the solution was at hand. With much frowning and looks of disdain, the camp commander listened to my pleas of feeling unwell and drove me to the train that took me to my favourite aunt's place in Melbourne.

The other remaining element in what transpired to be a not very successful religious education was Religious Instruction in primary school. I think I understood why it was called Religious Instruction and not Religious Education because we didn't learn much. It was conducted once a week for all of us Protestant kids by the Lutheran church. Unlike other denominations – if laying claims to their own church was to be seen as proof – the Lutherans weren't on the best of terms with the Maker. They had no church building of their own and had to make do with rented space in the Memorial Hall. Admittedly, the Germans made the mistake of being on the wrong side in two wars, but this deprivation of a house of worship seemed to be carrying hostilities a bit far. After all, the district contained lots of families with German names just like ours (Hampel): Zable, Turnitz, Richter, Nimmitz, Schonheim, Altman, Wally Jensz. I have included Wally Jensz's first name here out of deference to our special relationship with him. He moved into special friend territory when he allowed us to gorge ourselves on his mulberry tree and we staggered home with faces and hands stained and bucket full.

Mr Noak, the Lutheran pastor, got the gig for RI and mounted the classroom platform once a week. He was gaunt, seriously so – rather like Silo Jack. In fact, I cannot recall anyone in Walpeup who was not slender, aside from elderly Mrs Varney who was somewhat plump. She was distinguished not by her weight, but by the extensive reading she revealed during community singing quizzes. When Mr Noak spoke, his Adam's apple moved energetically up and down like a golf ball in an elastic stocking – quite the distracting spectacle. What pleased us was to see that on arrival, he had under his arm, his much-anticipated large roll of bible story pictures, each at least sixty centimetres in length. These were richly coloured stories of Lot's wife, the Good Samaritan, the Tower of Babel and Adam and Eve, heads bowed in guilt, driven out of their lovely garden home, and others. We waited in expectant silence as our instructor ceremoniously unrolled the picture for the week and our gaze swung momentarily away from the gyrations of his Adam's apple. Yet it was the colour, rather than any provocation to deep thought or religious feeling, that I found most captivating.

There was a secular context to my interest in these biblical charts. Not a lot of human-produced colour appeared in our lives at that time, and the natural environment of Walpeup contributed little. Compared with the huge range of autumn colours in North America and Europe, Mallee scrub was a monotonous olive green. Admittedly, tree trunks revealed some impressive colours – brown, orange, cream and white – but not the foliage. No blazing autumn displays in our scrub, only outbreaks of yellow when wattle bloomed.

Fashion and design had also not come to Walpeup. Almost as if art imitated nature, to wear reds, purples, bright blues or greens would be have been seen as flashy or suspicious. Colour in Mr Noak's charts therefore commanded attention, as did Jane Russell's provocative, sultry smile and generous curves on the poster in Mrs Dickie's shop window for the coming film *Outlaw*. It sent our pre-pubescent minds into riot, our first taste of colour enlisted in the aid of sex.

A decidedly more innocent display of colour was Lesley Rees's *Shy the Platypus*, a primary school book awarded to me, but that came earlier, before any adolescent stirrings. At that time, as throughout my school career, I was favoured by a lack of competition. Mostly we got awards just for turning up, in the scheme of things not the best way of fostering a realistic picture of one's abilities. On the cover, Shy, in grey-brown fur and black beak and claws, blew bubbles as he torpedoed down through crystalline blue and green waters. Using colour to entice readers, publishers were onto something. It was all the more novel for us in the absence of a library in school, or in the district.

It took a radio broadcast to complement Rees's images. In *Information Please* on Saturday evening 3WV, naturalist Crosbie Morrison led us on a journey through the natural world, including the paradox of an egg-laying creature with a duck bill. Conveniently, it came on after the round-up of country football scores, the progress of the major religion, and a rewarding double-billing.

Non-pecuniary Diversions

We enjoyed simple pleasures but never felt deprived. While I grew up with few books or toys, the timely arrival of a cricket bat – which we protected with linseed oil – and a junior-size steel rod with whiplash flexibility, told me that my parents looked after my interests. Plastic, and the oil used to make it, was largely non-existent and at least the oil for our cricket bat was a plant product. We even tried to make rings cut from toothbrush handles and the Perspex windows, so we believed, of aircraft. A prisoner of war would have been proud of our determination if not ingenuity.

I had a huge collection of cigarette boxes: Pall Mall, Lucky Strike, Camel, Big Ben, Ardath, Turf, Player's, Capstan, Craven A, Rothman's, Embassy and hundreds of others, all sufficiently colourful and different to sustain a flourishing trade among young kids. A supply chain was assured: by war's end some seventy per cent of Australian men smoked. Mum had her suspicions that I went beyond collecting. In my early primary years, she found tobacco in the top pocket of my shirt. I was not yet an accomplished dissembler, as my white shirt showed only too clearly.

A Meccano set inherited from Ian brought me up against limitations that have stayed with me. It assumed I would make things but took no account of my poor manual dexterity and limited spatial imagining. So deeply imbued with a desire to make things last, Ian had diligently and carefully oiled and cleaned his wind-up motor boat. As a result, I was fearful of doing it irreparable damage if I sailed it. Such concerns were not groundless because, already, use of even the most minimal technology presented problems for me.

Even at an early age, boredom pushed me to dip into my shallow well of creativity. I conceived a plan to trap a noisy miner, one of the native birds whose catholic appetite included the blossom of a sugar gum in our backyard. Like the cockroach, mouse or seagull, the annoying ever-squeaking bird's ability to draw sustenance from such diverse sources ensured its survival and abundance. I was determined to capture one by first putting enticing wheat on the ground beneath a wooden box propped up with a stick. To complete the operation, I attached stick to a long string, the other end of which I would hold from my position behind the house corner. Once the bird was seduced by the grain and underneath the box, I intended to pull on the string and trap it as the box fell. To me, a wonderfully simple scheme. As broad as the miner's tastes were, it treated the wheat with disdain and continued to wander noisily and contemptuously around the yard. To add insult to injury, barefooted, I trod on a bee, attracted like miners to the blossom, and went howling inside with its sting in my foot

I blame my lack of creativity on the fact that I was not an only child. Things were done for me, I guess. Harder still would be to explain my lack of manual dexterity and lack of any sign of technical competence. I couldn't blame my genes. Our paternal grandfather was a skilled woodworker. The intricate leafy patterns carved on the doors of our dining room sideboard attested to that. In fact, he made the whole edifice, with side shelves and both large and small mirrors on top. Similar carving on doors of a bedroom washstand made me wonder whether fine manual skills were more widespread in a previous era. Dad was no slouch either and inherited all his father's woodworking tools. The spokeshave, so named because of its use in rounding the spokes of wagon wheels, was one legacy. I watched how he stroked the sides of a sleek well-proportioned yacht made for us, about fifty centimetres long complete with keel, mast, sail and bowsprit. No ornament, it showed itself to be a working model on one of the nearby dams.

Television only arrived in 1956, by which time I had left the Mallee. Without it, we were free of the advertisements for consumer goods designed to remind us of our deprivation. Our wireless was permanently tuned to ABC 3WV and not commercial stations. I recall no incentive to ask why this was so. ABC announcers, almost all men, spoke with best British Received Pronunciation (RP). It was also a natural home when our very loyal royalist, Prime Minister Menzies, came on to address the nation. A good speaker himself, Dad admired this quality in the prime minister. More frequently on our Kriesler, the arresting, soaring, transporting voices of tenors Richard Tauber, Jussi Bjorling, Richard Crooks and Joseph Schmidt filled the kitchen. They seemed to have a special resonance with Mum. I thought, if only I could sing a fraction as well as they could. If only I could sing! Their effortlessness left me helpless, in near-tears.

Surely sopranos and contraltos also had their voices recorded. Less in favour in the ABC? Or I just tuned out? Gracie Fields I only remembered for 'The Biggest Aspidistra in the World', a slight piece for one who had an already established acting and singing career. In that era, gender discrimination was endemic and it would be surprising if it did not infiltrate elite cultural institutions like the ABC. On a lower plane, such was Dad's credibility as a witness on most things that for some time, I accepted his view that Bing Crosby was a moaner or groaner. My father never laid claim to any knowledge of music and, in retrospect, I suspect he was just being provocative. When at last I began thinking for myself, I felt that no one could evoke the spirit of Christmas like Bing. I couldn't get excited about nativity scenes but some hymns appealed to me, especially sung by Bing. In all, such a heritage left me conservative in taste and blissfully ignorant of popular culture.

It was Dad who provided the model of reading and although the few books given to me were magic, the initiative might have come from Mum. I remember vividly sitting in the rocking chair of my Aunt Moyna of the smoke-stained fingers and husky voice, reading my treasured *Winnie the Pooh*, my first real book. It struck a chord with me, especially Pooh lying in bed thinking about the honey he left in the pot at the bottom of a pit to catch heffalumps. Surely Milne was tapping a universal human trait. Who can resist that berry jam or cake of chocolate in the refrigerator? I can't. Another Christmas present was a slender book with the title *Warragul the Warrior* and its eponymous hero a dingo. Full marks for the writer's fidelity to Australian wildlife but it excited my imagination much less than Winnie's exploits and maybe a whiff of didacticism was no match for Milne's creativity and psychological insight. Both of these were abundant in May Gibbs's use of gum nuts and fearsome staring eyes of banksia men in *Snugglepot and Cuddlepie*. I would have strenuously argued that those banksia men were real. More than a homage to the Australian bush, it was a stroke of imaginative genius.

Older brother Ian's solution to our dearth of books was to give us *Raid on Heligoland*, printed shortly after war's end. Worthy was his desire to extend our intellectual horizons, but the language was university level when I was just experiencing the delights of basic literacy. So, sad to say, the book remained unread. I also never sought to sample the books arriving in a crate from the Council of Adult Education (CAE) while the group met under Dad's direction in our house. Normally, mischief if not curiosity would prompt me to do so. Maybe I just felt it was adult business.

What I did enjoy were those put out by the *Herald* newspaper in a sort of subscription list. Paul Brickhill's *The Great Escape* had the undoubted ring of authenticity because, previously imprisoned in Germany's Stalag Luft III, he was able to witness the daring escape attempt at first hand. He said that claustrophobia prevented his going down to excavate the tunnel himself. (Sounds like a good excuse but I believe him.) No wonder both his *The Dam Busters* and his account of Douglas Bader's heroic return, flying legless after a massive air crash, in *Reach for the Sky* were subsequently made into film. I learnt later that Norwegian Olaf Reed Olsen, author of *Two Eggs on my Plate*, had an equally adventurous and daring life during the war. These titles were about action, tailor-made for boys; and given my father's and brother's war service, and the recent emergence from World War II, I was obviously primed to enjoy them. Having said all this, my reading too often took a back seat to playing tennis, footy and cricket; gardening, bike riding, cutting and carting pine; and a range of domestic chores.

Some of the pleasure of my reading these books derived from the fact that it was shared with Dad. I knew nothing of his schooling beyond his mention of his gaining his Merit certificate but it seemed enough to set him on the reading path, not to the extent of pursuing it with abandonment but more as a source of quiet pleasure.

Communing With Nature

I could never forget that Walpeup was a small dot on the landscape surrounded by farmland and, importantly, by scrub. While my farm friends, the twins, were still attending their tiny school, hidden among the scrub and thus available only on weekends. I spent many hours wandering alone in the scrub surrounding Walpeup. Ostensibly looking for our cow, I was ever on the lookout for nests of birds whose eggs I'd not yet secured for my collection.

At this stage in my life, social encounters were a bit of a challenge so I didn't mind longish periods alone. Or was I so alone? Out in the bush, I was sometimes conscious of a censorious God monitoring my movements from above the clouds. If a sense of guilt was a desired outcome of religion, then perhaps Mum's efforts to keep me on the path of righteousness were working. Sometimes, the dirge of a wind soughing through the long string-like leaves of belah (casuarina) trees unsettled me and kindled my lingering insecurities. Paradoxically, it was also liberating to wander aimlessly and without obligation.

Most of the vegetation surrounding town was the stunted Mallee. It was a vegetation type that extended from south-west New South Wales, across north-western Victoria and into South Australia. While remarkably ignorant of its different varieties, I loved the flourishing bird life associated with it. For me, the birds were a source of delight, surprise and anticipation and a contradictory mixture of the material and the aesthetic. On one hand, collecting birds' eggs; on the other, marvelling at the richness of colour, sound and flight behaviour almost on our doorstep. I could readily name forty species. Deep into the scrub, a mournful chorus of rising and falling screeches told me of the presence of an extended family of jays (or white-winged choughs).

Black with white wing tips, they flapped noisily in unison away from their solid round mud nest. On their departure, the scrub gave over to the subtle twitter of blue wrens (superb fairy wrens) hopping joyfully about; excited chatter of willy wagtails, tails in perpetual motion like metronomes; galahs raucously emerging from a hollow to settle high in the trees; fairy martins cavorting in pursuit of insects overhead; the ring-necked parrot, a flash of green and yellow darting through the foliage; and always in the distance, the long mournful descending 'caark' of crows (or what I learned later were ravens!).

One day, something startled me. Approaching an old hollow tree, I heard a rustling inside. A flat white face with crooked beak emerged, followed by loud scratching of powerful claws. A cream and brown barn owl stretched its wings and swooped away in a long downward parabola. Reaching its nadir, it let loose a stream of white poo, like thick gossamer trailing behind it. Its soft plumage produced a flight that was stealthy and soundless, ideal for swooping onto unsuspecting mice.

We sometimes saw a tawny frogmouth, no relation of a barn owl despite its appearance, and not the epitome of avian beauty, sitting motionless, silhouetted on a limb near nightfall or doing a double act as a dead log. Their relations, owlet nightjars, we saw rarely.

Dusk had its particular accompaniment. While Dad and I sat on the post office steps during an approaching storm, we heard the cadence of a pair of lonely spur-winged plovers floating on the wind and disappearing into the night air as they circled over the golf course outside town. With night fallen, silence. More commonly, after the last wheat truck had driven home, we listened to the slow, mournful and repetitive call of the mopoke somewhere in the darkened scrub.

A bird that always appeared to me to be the epitome of innocence, industry and beauty was the swallow. Occasionally, we found them darting back and forth with astonishing agility around deserted farmhouses. They gave a short shrill squeak as they caught insects on the wing and returned them to their young, secure in patiently moulded mud nests under the eaves.

Then there were the solitary blue cranes, what I was to learn much later were in fact white-faced herons. Australia has two cranes, the brolga and sarus, waist-high birds, neither of which I saw around Walpeup. If we were quiet and sneaked up on one of the many dams filled from those Grampians storages, we might find a solitary grey and white blue crane, taking measured steps in the shallows, its long neck stretched to search for yabbies. Its omnivorous habits should have helped its survival but abandonment of open channels, use of pipes and consequent loss of dams have not treated them well.

Regrettably, baiting of vermin, spraying of insecticides and herbicides and loss of habitat all contributed to the decline of many bird species. The depredations in the Mallee were but a part of the nationwide loss of biodiversity. The downside of getting old is that one has personally borne witness to it.

The Perks of Being 'Disadvantaged'

Not all of my youth was spent in blissful and contented isolation. My mother took me as a very young child to sample Melbourne's pleasures. Farewelling Dad, we waited on Ouyen station while Mildura passengers, still energised, bought a pie in the railway cafeteria. Our mother, Bruce and I lumbered our cases along the corridor of the second-class carriage, checking numbers in each compartment. We found ours and an obliging fellow occupant lifted our case onto the netting racks. To me, the other five travellers were too old to make interesting conversation and, happily, they settled into silence. Unable to sleep, as the night dragged on, I found the padded green seats and grim black and white framed photographs above us oppressive. I poked my head out the lift-up window but quickly withdrew, my face blackened with coal dust and smoke. Finally, sleep-deprived, we arrived at Spencer Street Station and caught a cab to Auntie Jean's.

It took little time to realise that not only would banging into the nearest dodgem car at Luna Park not incur damage, it was expected, and it was huge fun. Bruce and I paused, captivated by our distorted images in bended glass mirrors, then we zoomed to the bottom of the big slide. Soon, I realised the foolishness of venturing onto the slide with built-in hills and troughs. My head rising and falling uncontrollably, I slumped bawling at the bottom, bottom lip now bloody and stinging. All the bravado on the dodgems vanished.

In town, the pantomime *Peter Pan* was magic. Gravity-defying fairies descended like gossamer, suspended on barely visible wire. Was it at this performance that a man beating out stirring notes on a Wurlitzer rose from the underworld? It might have been at Disney's movie of delicate little fawn *Bambi*. It evoked every ounce of empathy

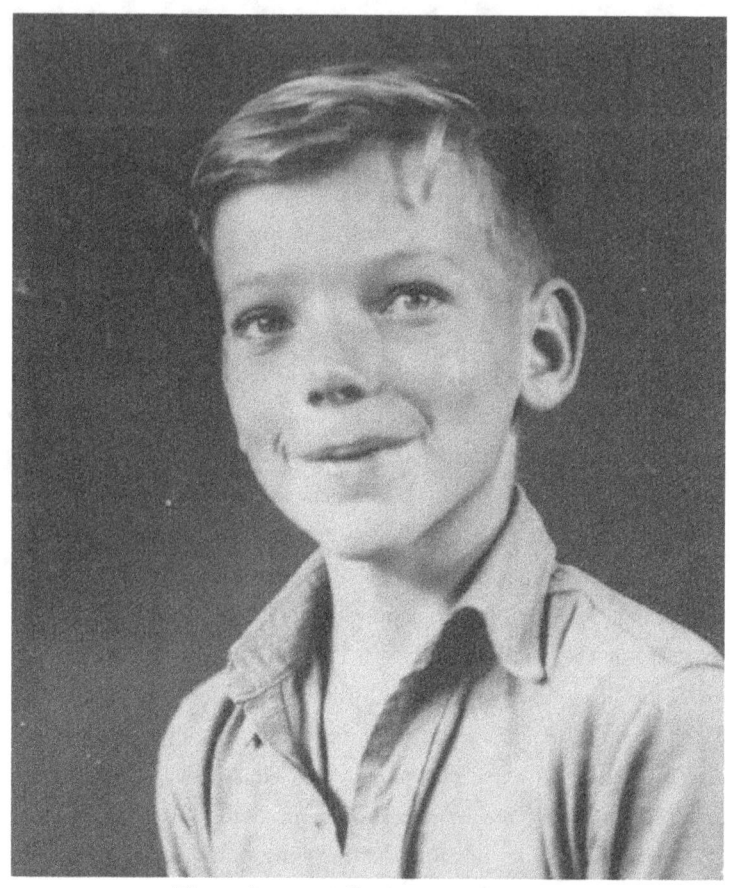

The author at Mallee Boys' Camp, 1949.

and fear I had. Disney brought together the sort of entrancing image, colour and music he did in *The Sorcerer's Apprentice*, which I was only to see much later.

These were highlights of a barely remembered infancy. A bigger departure from rural life came when I was about ten. It was an era when, in the race of life, boys had the inside running. By virtue of its remoteness, the Mallee was still deemed a disadvantaged area and its youth therefore qualified for a camp by the seaside, called the Mallee Boys' Holiday Camp at Portsea. That girls might have similar needs was a thought that somehow never arose. Housed in several galvanised-iron ex-army Nissen huts, the Portsea affair was a sort of Butlin's without sideshow attractions. For me, it was a mixed experience.

When we parked our bags on double bunks, I was grateful that more confident individuals held the floor amid anecdotes and jockeying for attention. Gatherings of this size didn't exist at Walpeup. That evening, in an improvised Carnegie Hall, I again found myself among lots of boys united by their apparent familiarity with a strange song. This time, not Happy Clappy rejoicing by the fervent young people at a Bible-basher's camp. The assembled lads launched forth into a repetitive, but to them, meaningful piece. It sounded something like 'Ging Gang Gooly Gooly Watcha, Ging Gang Goo. Ging Gang Goo. Helah, oh Helah Shelah'. Totally incomprehensible to me. What was worse, they chorused it with enthusiasm equal to that of God-blessed young people up in the hills east of Melbourne. I soon realised it was part of the arcane language and rituals of Boy Scouts, an organisation which didn't exist in Walpeup. What it did mean was that I was again the outsider, a feeling that no insecure young boy wants to admit.

One of the small treats of the camp was being able, on an aircraft beached on the sands, to reprise World War II, which had ended a mere four years before. It seemed to be a flying boat. Its undamaged fuselage was either a stroke of genius by camp organisers or evidence of a pilot's poor flying, but we didn't enquire. Its presence led us to wonder whether the navigator was too absorbed in enjoying his Violet Crumble and had lost concentration. One of the boys related with due authority that there was flying boat base on Lake Boga to the north of the state near Swan Hill. Whatever its origins, cockpit open, perspex windscreen intact, we could sit and fly into our imagination. Noisy, dominant kids immediately assumed the role of pilot and navigator, I and more retiring ones relegated to bringing up supplies of ammunition.

A bigger treat that required less imaginative challenge was a cruise up Port Phillip Bay on a corvette, a sleek, grey and menacing vessel with a bold black identification number emblazoned on its side. Excitement was high because matters military had an abiding fascination for me. We boarded across a wavering gangplank, comforted by the presence of ropes to grasp and the close attention of two sailors in absurdly laundered and pressed white suits. On board, mooring rope withdrawn and engines vibrating with power, I found the four-inch (102-millimetre) cannons and 1.5-inch (forty-millimetre) pom pom an exciting reminder that this was the real stuff.

An officer explained the corvette's capabilities. 'She's a little over 1,000 tons and 180 feet long. Flat out, she'll go fifteen knots or just over seventeen miles an hour. In addition to the pom poms you can see, the other, smaller ones, fore and aft are machine guns. We also have depth charges. In wartime, we mostly go looking for mines and submarines.'

My imaginary shooting down enemy planes was cut short. Unaccountable yawning was the first sign of what I feared – seasickness. I felt embarrassed because we were experiencing no more than a benign swell and more so because other kids were excitedly pointing out buildings they recognised as we voyaged along the southern suburbs of Port Phillip Bay. I was determined not to throw up. By standing at the rail, facing the wind with mouth open and blocking my nostrils to the nauseating mixture of diesel and galley smells, I could stop my stomach surging up to my mouth. When diesel fumes had come from Zable's powerful tractor hauling a load to the silo, they never bothered me, but this was a different combination. The only thing threatening to fill my mouth now was not masticated wheat but something less pleasant. In this manner, I managed to hold off until mercifully we landed. For the next two days, with every step, the ground disconcertingly kept rising and falling.

As members of the underprivileged at the Mallee boys' camp, we were also given a medical check-up, a sort of 5,000-mile service for nine to thirteen-year-olds. Back home, nineteen miles (thirty kilometres) of gravel road separated us from Dr Nihill's surgery in Ouyen. Other boys were almost certainly equally remote from medical facilities. Timidly, I stepped into one of the spartan ex-army Nissen huts serving as a medical centre. When called, I left several boys sitting waiting at the entrance and nervously followed the signs into the first room.

The first nurse had a speech impediment and the energy of someone starting her shift. She asked me 'to cloth my eyes, bring the paper clother to thee if I you can put the bird into the cage drawn on a peeth of paper. Mm,' she said, 'you probably need to strengthen thoth eye muthles. Glathes will fickth them.'

Images of trying to play footy with glasses on flashed through my mind.

I didn't realise how prescient she was. Three years of almost daily headaches and nausea meant I could defer further eye testing and glasses no longer. I was condemned to wearing spectacles with circular lenses framed in thin tortoiseshell. Henceforth, kids dubbed me Herman Whizzer. I guessed it came from a comic that I had somehow missed and I knew the label was not complimentary.

This was not a relaxing start to my holiday. The next encounter was totally predictable. I had already endured face-numbing hours at the Red Cliffs dentist. I had no doubt I was not winning the war against tooth decay and was not desperate to face further ignominy. Bad news was only too predictable. This time it came from a short, balding man whose air of blasé indifference immediately set me on the defensive. What about a bit of sympathy? I asked myself.

Finally, I was ushered into the presence of a nurse and an expectation of a more gentle judgement. I will admit that her curvaceous figure, high cheekbones and whiff of exotic perfume disarmed me. No elaborate equipment, just a picture on the wall of a body's entanglement of sinews and muscles, a set of scales and markings and accompanying heights up the wall. My weight taken, I jumped at her request to stand erect against the markings. She swished a ruler up and down between back and wall, and pronounced with some gravity that I was sway-backed. Shaken, I looked at her quizzically, but feeling I needed no confirmation that I was not Adonis. I could press my backside and shoulders to the wall as instructed, but my back would not go closer.

Finally she examined my feet. 'You're flat-footed. Do you run much?' she asked gently with an implication too obvious to ignore.

Such an accumulated assault on the self-esteem was not something I was prepared for.

As I walked back along the corridor, past the next ones sitting waiting, one of them asked, 'How'd yer go?'

'Fine. No worries,' I said.

A couple of years later, at the age of thirteen and in Form Three (Year Nine), I managed to put aside growing test anxiety to sit a general knowledge examination. It was a preliminary selection procedure for what was then known as the *Sun Advertiser* Youth Travel (SAYT). *The Sun News Pictorial* might not have been God's gift to literature but its executives deserved brownie points for their initiative. In a display of interstate amity, they joined forces with the Adelaide *Advertiser* to sponsor a schoolboys' trip abroad. As in the couple of years before 1953, it would plan and organise a sea voyage to England then a two-month bus tour of the British Isles. My interest had been aroused by a boy in my class, a year older than I was, who had been regaling us with tales of his SAYT trip. A clever kid, he decided that later, in our Matriculation year when he and I were the last of our original Form 1 (Year 7) class of '44, shooting foxes and running a farm held out prospect of more immediate excitement and long-term financial reward than studies. The consequences for his exam results were not good.

It became clear to me that being an underprivileged rural kid had its upside. Although a couple of charitable organisations sponsored boys, including that of world billiards champion for seventeen years, Walter Lindrum, the initial criterion for selection for the SAYT was the shire in which one lived. The gods beamed down on me because Walpeup Shire was the most sparsely populated one in the state. This meant fewer boys and less opposition. The written general knowledge test was designed to select a group of finalists. Very democratically, they called for interview in the Shire Hall in Ouyen three boys from Ouyen and three from Murrayville at the western end of the municipality. The mayor, a representative of the *Sun* newspaper and a local resident were lined up on the other side of a large table, their reflections mirrored in its surface. At first, I felt one lot of inquisitors was enough for me without the reflections. Still, I regained my composure and nascent cunning or acquired competitiveness took over. I realised that if I talked up, my chances of being selected would be enhanced. To my good fortune, the topic for discussion was myxomatosis in rabbits. As one who had a thriving little money spinner trapping rabbits before the depredations of the virus myxomatosis, I did have a ready supply of comments and a competitive determination that they would be heard. This was a challenge because I had been told at home that it was impolite to talk over anyone.

It was prearranged that I would phone my mother to announce the result of the interview. I began by telling her how many boys were finalists and the questions we were asked.

She interrupted with a 'Come on. Who won?'

'I did,' I said. No whooping with joy. No incoherent and triumphant jumble of words, just the 'I did'.

One war that Mum constantly waged was the war on skites or blabbermouths. Undoubtedly, self-aggrandisement is not an attractive feature in anybody but one of the effects of these frequent admonitions was that a healthy pride in my achievements and healthy self-esteem became illegitimate traits. How much this was a psychological component of the tall poppy syndrome reaching into rural areas and how much a vestige of living in a basically egalitarian community is hard to say. Who knows? Mum might have been betraying her own lack of confidence. It is possible that such a prohibition on self-displays had the reverse effect on me and this often played out in high school, to the frustration of several teachers.

Horizons Expanded

I had been on an overnight steam train visit to Melbourne a couple of times but sailing for the British Isles, or home as it was then regarded, promised to be a significant change of pace and perspective for me. Initially, it also brought unforgettable discomfort.

With farewells from the state governor, state premier and family, streamers, a toilet roll and a ball of string finally severed, we glided out into the bay. For nearly three days, we buffeted our way across the Great Australian Bight. For too much of that time, Graeme Herde and I sat on top deck by the *Oronsay*'s swimming pool, too sick to move or hold down even a dry biscuit. Each time the ship pitched riotously, the stern rose, propellers flailed vainly in the air, and the whole stern juddered. Herde and I sat anchored like kittens after an abortive drowning, drenched and blinking while swimming pool contents sloshed up over us then returned for another assault. In other circumstances, it might have been fun. A welcome distraction for over an hour were two large grey and white albatrosses gliding over the white caps. Absolute masters of the elements, soaring and diving effortlessly, they mocked our enslavement by the storm.

I had become acquainted with the *Oronsay*'s propellers. Sharing a cabin down on H deck, we had to get used to the throb of the propeller shaft. It was driven by a 42,000-horsepower motor, dwarfing anything I had seen or heard. After the sluggishness of the corvette, the twenty-six-knot (forty-eight-kilometre-per-hour) speed of *Oronsay* seemed wondrously fast for a vessel thirty times the corvette's tonnage. Even so, it was still only about a quarter the size of modern cruise liners.

When once Herde and I made a tentative foray into the dining room, his complexion still bore signs of his nausea.

The author with the Governor of Victoria, 1953.

Neville graciously pointed out the tonal similarity between a serving of pale green pistachio ice cream and the face of my fellow sufferer, exclaiming loudly, 'Herde!'

This wasn't what I had in mind for a four-month trip abroad. I had forgotten the corvette trip and should have taken notice of the ominous signs as we first sailed towards the heads of Port Phillip Bay. But what could I have done? I stood at the rail in Fremantle before disembarking for a brief stopover, determined to head back home – by train. I concluded there was no getting around it. I'd get seasick crossing a wet lawn and the thousands of sea miles ahead were not an attractive prospect. The smell of the ship's corridors took on an almost physical presence that stayed with me for years.

Someone must have dangled some sort of bait before me – food, most likely. Perhaps also the windless, sunny skies and millpond Indian Ocean tipped the scales. The sea sparkled and, despite gnawing hunger, my spirits lifted. We had a lot of catching up to do. For the next five days, we ploughed through breakfast, lined up for morning ice cream, tried every course on *Oronsay*'s lunch menu down to biscuits and cheese, jostled for lead position ready for door opening at afternoon tea, then at

"Pledge your loyalty to Queen" — GOVERNOR TELLS SUN TOUR BOYS

"AS the Queen in Westminster Abbey dedicates herself to her Empire, so must you lads dedicate yourselves to our Queen," the Governor (Sir Dallas Brooks) said in his farewell to the 33 Sun Youth Travel boys on the Oronsay yesterday.

The boys listened intently as Sir Dallas told them what they would see at the Coronation, what they should do in England, and what they should tell the people they met.

The Governor farewelled the boys on the games deck.

The general manager of The Sun (Mr. F. Packer), the editor (Mr. J. C. Waters) and the Oronsay's captain listened to him advising the boys.

The games deck was crowded with more than 300 hundred parents, relatives and friends of the Coronation contingent.

The boys will make a four-month educational tour of England and Scotland, with the chief of staff of The Sun (Mr. Keith Cairns), who is director of the contingent.

Highlight of the tour will come on June 2 when the boys will cheer the Queen from Parliament Place, London, as she enters Westminster Abbey.

More joining

Twenty more boys will join the ship at Adelaide. Of the 33 who sailed yesterday 31 were Victorians and two Tasmanians.

The Governor said that the trip was a "great venture." He told the boys to remember with gratitude that The Sun had made it possible.

They could show their gratitude by telling the people of England about Australia's fine cities, grand way of life and limitless future, he said.

"Proudly tell them the truth about your great country and persuade them to come and settle here," he said.

...said that at the Coronation they would see ceremony and pageantry unequalled in the world. They would be "stunned by its magnificence."

In the Abbey

"Inside the Abbey the Queen takes part in the most significant part of the Coronation — the most historic religious ceremony in the world," he said.

"She will dedicate herself to the Empire, and you boys should dedicate yourselves to her."

Sir Dallas told the boys they were Australian ambassadors.

The Queen would be coming to Australia soon after her Coronation, and the Youth contingent should try to tell every Englishman what sort of country the Queen would be going to.

Then he said: "I think you should applaud The Sun for making all this possible."

Sir Dallas was given three cheers as he left.

Earlier the contingent was farewelled by the Lord Mayor (Cr. Brens).

He gave them the freedom of the city's motto — Vires Asquirit Eundo, and translated it — "We gather strength as we go."

He said that he hoped it would apply to their travels.

"You have been selected for qualities and attributes that place you above other boys," Cr. Brens said.

"You are going away as trustees of a great country and of your respective municipalities.

"Seek knowledge and find the channels through which you can best express your individualities. Seek the work that is going to give you pleasure.

"You will do better work that way, because vocation and pleasure go hand in hand."

Cr. Brens paid tribute to The Sun "for the very grand thought that prompted it to give an opportunity for you lads to tour abroad."

"We are indebted to an organisation such as The Sun, so public-minded, so public-spirited as to give that opportunity," he said.

The Town Clerk (Mr. Wootton) telling the boys something of the City Council's work and of what they would see in England, said he had been proud of the way in which Sun Youth boys had conducted themselves in England in 1951, when he saw them there.

"It showed the good upbringing of the boys and very good training by Mr. Moloney" (Sun Youth Travel director), he said.

"Mr. Moloney has done an extraordinarily fine job and his prestige is very high in England."

"Seal of city"

Mr. J. F. Williams, managing editor of The Sun and the Herald & Weekly Times Ltd., responding to the praise of Sun Youth Travel, thanked the Lord Mayor and Mr. Wootton for arranging the reception.

It set the seal of the City on the tour, he said.

He expressed particular gratitude to Cr. Brens for speaking to the boys although so recently back from his strenuous visit to Australian troops in Korea.

"Everyone in Melbourne is proud that the Lord Mayor of Melbourne has displayed the City's interest to the men, who have not seen a great deal of people from their home land," Mr. Williams said.

Departure instructions, 1953.

more sober pace, enjoyed a gourmet meal in the evening. The Tourist B menu for Monday, 4 May 1953 began: Potage Egyptienne, Gnocchis, Milanaise, Pariisienne Steaks, Lyonnaise, Corned Pork, Parsley Sauce, and continued down through several items to Fruit Sandwich Pastry; Sao Biscuits; Cheddar and Gorgonzola Cheese Pickles. Did we need to travel? We had it all there on the menu. Unused to such prodigality, we thought it was our duty to work through the menu item by item. The evidence to the contrary was the perplexed response by our waiter with the very large dent in his head. Had he, like Charlie, the former farm hand, also failed to notice a horse's kick coming? There seemed to be a connection between our waiter's indentation and his refusal to speak. When we gave our order, he'd stand unsmiling, perplexed, then wheel around and head for the scullery.

Victorian Premier John Cain dropped in from first class. So, after appearing in photos with us on departure, he had stayed on board after all! In an act of noblesse oblige, he gave us Victorian travellers ten pounds to share. Our contingent manager, Keith Cairns, was also general manager of the *Sun* newspaper. His mission was to get ideas from Britain and the US for the eventual opening of TV in our state, HSV7 in 1956, in time for the Olympic Games.

It is hard to overstate the extent to which the British Isles and royalty had been embedded in our consciousness. As said, the pull of home was still strong. In this era of democratic air travel, any touristic account of a UK trip over sixty years ago is bound to be a cliché. Nevertheless, two months of sea travel with stopovers in ports so stunningly culturally and economically different in the company of fifty-two other fourteen to sixteen-year-olds (I was the youngest), three teachers, and two months bussing around England and Scotland, shook up my horizons. It would be an understatement to say that there could have been no greater contrast between this trip and the experience of sitting with Dad on our post office steps, our voices the only sound in the encroaching darkness.

Not many Australians would be so close to a coronation. We stood in a reserved place outside Westminster Abbey with its bells triumphantly pealing out. We could hear clearly the thin, high-pitched aristocratic tones of a young Queen over loud speakers. Guards marched by in lock-step, helmets gleaming. Seeing their packaged lunch delivered where they stood raised the question whether an exceptionally large bladder was a selection criterion for guard service. The Queen of Tonga, Menzies, Churchill and other royals and prime ministers sailed pompously by in fairyland coaches.

Few have the luxury of being billeted in so many homes to sample still flourishing accents and generous hospitality. Admittedly for breakfast the first day, at the home of a widowed Londoner, I got a shock to be served two lonely smoked kippers sitting forlornly on my plate. Equally surprising was the idea of taking a bath in a tub brought into the lounge room. My hostess had never travelled more than eight miles out of London yet she generously offered what she had. It included the chance to walk the corridors at the back of Buckingham Palace, where she was a cleaner. I still see footmen with funny leggings, wig in a bun and powdered faces – or again, media images playing tricks on the memory?

My hostess took time out to walk me around London. A bomb site, rubble intact but turned into a park, reminded me how much the city suffered in the devastating explosions and fires from mid-1940 to September 1941. I later learned that about a million houses were destroyed and over 20,000 killed in the capital alone, including, as mentioned, my uncle, his wife and one of their two sons.

Driving around in two buses, we passed by millennia of history enshrined in ceremonies and museums and buildings humble and grandiose. 'Ships, towers, domes, theatres, temples lie. Open unto the fields and to the skies': the poets have said it all before and with an eloquence few can aspire to. Impressions jostling in the mosaic of our memories: centuries-old suits of armour symbolising class, royalty and struggles for power; pelletised grass fed to cosseted Scottish dairy cows; gleaming salmon in highland streams; bottomless Loch Ness; tales of Alexander Graeme Bell; Dali's dramatic foreshortened painting of Christ in Glasgow art gallery; lunch at St Andrews golf course; embarrassment at an attempt to demonstrate boomerang throwing to my Nottingham hosts (it landed wedged in a tree); a miniature English village built to one-ninth scale; Anne Hathaway's cottage; Gray's immortal lines, 'The plowman homeward plods his weary way' on a tomb; mesmerised by the wizardry of Harlem Globetrotters on TV; and buying my mother a pair of Sheffield stainless steel hedge clippers for a hedge we were never likely to have. So much packed into those two months.

We had brief bits of recreation within a trip that was basically tourism with an educative bent. One diversion was a cricket match in which older, bigger and more skilled members of our contingent played a leading Scottish college. We lost. More memorable for me was the photographic record of old boys who were killed in both wars. Back home, just about to reach the meteoric heights of high school status, Ouyen Higher Elementary had no such unenviable heritage.

Rather than defeat on the sports or battlefield, a dance in a Crieff girls' school meant that lesser lights such as I did not have to stand on the sidelines. My attempts at dancing remain forgettable but one girl, clearly older than I, gave me an especially warm cheerio as our bus departed. Was I presenting as a baby brother needing encouragement? Or was she shy and my unsophisticated bearing presented her as unthreatening and no cause for discomfort? Maybe she was just glad to see me go and relieved of responsibility. If the organisers wanted us all to feel important, they succeeded. My diary tells me she was nice.

Even the eight weeks plus of sea travel with brief visits to watch snake charmers and cobra with teeth drawn, energetic vendors in bumboats, steaming tropical millions, being transported in buses with driver's hand perpetually on the horn, red stains of betel juice, fragrance of frangipani, the passing parade along Suez Canal – before the crisis of 1956 – all assaulted the senses. Such memories are embedded in the teak elephant bookends I bought in Colombo and now sitting on my mantelpiece.

The relative absence of photos to document my childhood before I turned fourteen, all changed with the SAYT trip. It started with the newspaper shot of us, fresh-faced lads crowding eagerly around Sir Dallas Brooks, Victorian Governor. In a photo on deck of all fifty-three, we looked, by today's standards, like inmates released from a concentration camp. Takeaway food was in the future. My parents paid for my camera, a folding specimen that left a legacy of some fifty small black and white images.

Two incidents on that trip are worth recalling because they suggest that we were just as capable of *Schadenfreude* as youth today.

The first occurred during our brief stopover at Aden in what is today Yemen. Before the ship anchored, skinny urchins breaststroked and trod water, eyes scanning the ship. With bottoms up in the air like wild ducks after morsels on a lake floor, they dived to retrieve passengers' coins before their target see-sawed to the bottom. As our ship pulled out of the harbour, one of our party still held the string designed to convey purchases up to the ship from the hawker in his bumboat. The practice was that money had to be sent back in return. Indecision perhaps but it was clear that the pedlar was not going to see his stuffed camel again or the money paid for it. As our departing vessel gathered speed, and he tried to keep up with us, the poor man's rowing and gesticulations increased in a frantic syncopation. The string broke and, accepting that this was one sale he'd not make, he stopped rowing and sagged on his oars. Our last sight was of a lone figure merging into silhouette, shaking a last fist in anger. Defeated, he turned for shore.

The other took place on a desolate windswept ridge in the Scottish Highlands. A solitary piper stood erect in full kilt outfit at the edge of the road, his bagpipes hanging from his right hand. On sighting our two buses approaching, he sprang into life, raised his instrument and, cheeks reddening with exertion and the biting wind, he began playing 'Scotland the Brave' with all the patriotic fervour he could muster. We piled out, took our photos, climbed back in and the buses drove off. As he faded in the distance, we saw the highlander shaking his head, having not earned a penny. To my shame now, I joined in the chorus of laughter as we continued the winding Highlands journey.

In the promise of getting a prize – forlorn in my case – we sought to cement our experiences in a diary. I also contracted to write letters to the *Ouyen and District Northwest Express* to fulfil an unexpressed obligation to the shire. For reasons of temperament or just that correctness took priority over creativity at school, my pieces were grammatically unchallenged but absolutely no help to paper's sales.

Adjustment to life back at school might have been difficult were it not for desultory study attempts on board *Oronsay* on the trip over and *Strathnaver* on return. Even they were interrupted. When a ship passed, some boys saw fit to launch into declamations about its origin, cargo, speed, destination – anything to demonstrate their knowledge. After all, not only were we young, but it was performance in two tests of knowledge that was indisputable evidence that we were of special stuff. For all our self-puffery, we were stunned into silence by flying fish launching metres into the air, darting with fins fluttering like wind-up toys about eighty metres across the surface then plopping back into the waves. Keeping pace with us, dolphins provided a brief escort as they arched gracefully in and out of the water. But these could not hold us for ever because morning ice cream beckoned.

One of the treats especially designed for boys was a trip to the bridge and the chance to take hold of the helm. It might have been nervousness or the overpowering impulse to have an effect but I was obviously too energetic. I gave the wheel a vigorous turn and the ship heeled over noticeably, all 29,000 tons of it. Elevated as we were, the effect was also probably magnified. It wasn't the first time I was acutely embarrassed by my excesses and was only too relieved to pass control back to the first officer who, to his credit, smiled and remained silent. I was even rewarded on descent for my impetuosity with ice cream handed out to us all.

Apart from the scourge of seasickness, we enjoyed good health throughout the trip. Before departure on this grand adventure, we had obligatory injections against typhoid, cholera and smallpox. No protest at the nanny state there, not even at Dr Nihill's gruff exterior.

Primary School Had Its Challenges

For some reason, my memories of the period before school are faint. In fact, I have almost none. Reputedly we are supposed to be able to recall events from the age of three. It's a facility probably tied up with language development. In the absence of any evidence that I had been brutalised and had suppressed several years' of living, my excuse is that I had no store of photos on which to hang my recollections. At most, there were half a dozen of me by high school age, or so I thought. Perhaps I felt I was important enough to be deserving of more.

If the developing human organism thrives on stimulation, where did it come from during those nearly five preschool years? There was no preschool, no TV and therefore no *Sesame Street* or *Play School*. In the company of parents, life was about tagging along to local events; being driven about; looking at a fearsome coloured picture book about pirates; lots of physical play but little of the intellectual sort; early induction into chores and guilt; watching Dad in the garden, milking and building the boat. In almost all of these, I was a passive onlooker, a metaphorical and sometimes literal passenger, mostly unchallenged except to heed maternal commands. All of this could be excuse, for there was always the option of seeking my own stimulation and no doubt the genuinely curious would do that.

Just before my fifth birthday in late February, Mum sent me to primary school, perhaps in a desire to be relieved of a querulous kid. I had no insight into the extent to which my parents shared such decisions. It was 1944, the year before the end of conflict in Europe. Once it was all over and soldiers returned, many women previously gainfully employed in the war effort were now ushered back into domesticity. Mostly, there was no such occupational transition

The author, left back, primary school party, 1946.

for rural women. Post-war was the beginning of great economic expansion, something of great advantage to anyone later employed as a teacher, especially if one were warm blooded, male and vertical. Both my primary and secondary schools were in transition. The former was shedding its Grades 7 and 8 and the latter moving into the '50s, with the addition of Forms 5 and 6, thus being a regular high school, albeit with one of the smallest enrolments in the state.

Sometimes in a small rural school, the wife of the head teacher could be recruited for a role presumed to require more motherly skills. In our school, it meant responsibility for new entrants and using her capacity to hold a tune. Mrs Monaghan was undoubtedly sensitive to the needs of the timorous first graders but she was also associated for ever in my mind over the next couple of years with her singing, particularly of the lilting, sad, South African song 'Sarie Marais'. We did not attempt the Afrikaans version nor did we fully appreciate the song's nostalgic patriotism, but in English, its melody appealed to us immensely.

Every primary school had a flagpole, its use the first inculcation of obedience. Monday mornings began with a saluting the flag ceremony and expression of allegiance to a distant king. Little choppers standing in line, the breeze whistling around bare legs, raised their right hand to their forehead as a monitor tugged the flag to the top. At teacher's prompting, we all recited the oath: 'I love God and my country. I honour the flag. I will serve the King and cheerfully obey my parents, teachers and the law.' It was never made clear exactly how we might serve a king 12,000 miles away but at least the virtue of obedience was not lost on us. Happily, we knew nothing about the Windsors' flirting with the German with the funny moustache who had already revealed himself to be not a very nice chap. Nevertheless, for the most part, we showed unfailing loyalty except when cheerfully came out as chiefly. Meanwhile, the war was not yet over; Dresden was being firebombed with huge destruction and, some argue, unnecessary loss of life.

So much of my schooling seemed to place inestimable value on absorption, rote and repetition. It was not apparent to me at the time why we learnt times tables, for example, although as time wore on, I could see the benefit. Self-discovery was at a minimum. Curiosity was something kids brought to school but, from then on, was at best an irrelevant distraction or, at worst, something to be suppressed. I did not know how to learn and, for most of my schooling, it did not occur to teachers that this was something useful to impart. At the outset, my feeble efforts were recorded on a slate, without frame, so rough around the edges it could have been ripped from the nearest roof. Then came pencil and subsequently steel-nibbed pens which we dipped into little porcelain inkwells recessed into the right-hand side of each desk. Bad luck for the ten per cent born as left-handers. In some schools, left-handedness was a bad habit to be eradicated with a rap over the knuckles. We spent many hours laboriously furrowing nib into paper. In the process, as we tried to confine our scrawls between lines of work books, ink often accidentally flicked over the back of the kid in front. The civilising nature of good handwriting was apparently not to be underestimated. Being ink monitor brought a sense of importance but at the cost of ink stains all over hands that long outlasted the kid's tenure in the job.

In the interests of bringing literacy to the masses, every Victorian elementary school child had a Grade Reader. As the name implies, language and subject matter expanded with each elevation. We trotted out the reader for our daily mental and emotional training like a form of gymnastics. One of the stories seemed designed to impress us with Aboriginal ingenuity. Living in the bush as I was, the concept of living off the land had great appeal. I was captivated by the depiction of an Aborigine crouching beneath the surface of a lagoon and breathing through a straw until an unsuspecting duck paddled overhead and could be pulled by the leg and drowned.

I could never understand the intent of some of the other stories. The Hobyahs, for example, were fearsome black humanoid creatures that came run, run, running, skip, skip, skipping through the woods on some directionless but scary mission. It has to be remembered that these stories pre-dated political correctness. Lazy Tok would simply not pass the thought police today. Her story was illustrated by a very fat – who would now be classified obese – woman in a polka dot dress and slip-on sandals, fleeing a hive of bees strung out behind her in hot pursuit. The unappealing staccato sound of Tok and the epithet Lazy for some time cemented the idea that overweight people are necessarily lazy. And of course, not surprisingly, the figure of fun a woman.

As we rose to the stratospheric heights of Sixth Grade, the Reader was supplemented by an unbound monthly *School Paper* containing a mixture of a few contemporary issues, poems and always on the back, the words and music of a song. The lyrics, I'm afraid, were never more than decorative.

Walpeup primary school's facilities were basic: no plush gymnasium, no sports centre, no lunch room. But we did have a set of pigeonholes at the entrance in which we stored our drinking mugs. Mine was a yellow one, steel with chipped porcelain exterior and the words Made in Czechoslovakia clearly on the bottom. My mastery of that long word was a sign to me that I was on the path to greatness. No tribute to brilliance that I was called on to read to younger grades. It was, after all, a time-honoured practice in small rural schools and, to a degree, embodied the laudable principle of cross-age tutoring in which practice both tutor and tutored benefited. Mostly adopted, I fear, to give the teacher a break.

With summer temperatures hovering around a century Fahrenheit, access to cool drinking water was desirable. Our school water bag was a cylindrical sack dangling in the breeze from the peppercorn tree, a precursor to the water cooler without the workplace gossip. As with the Coolgardie safe, it was testament to the fact that, when temperatures were often above the century, the cooling potential of the breeze could and must be utilised. Our water bag had a top to it, fortunately, because caterpillars had a liking for the upper branches of the same tree. Slaking our thirst tended to be done on the run because the contents spilling from their spiderweb-like nests above caused an itch. Peppercorn trees were of Peruvian origin, their seeds brought out by gold-seekers in the mid-nineteenth century. These trees were a familiar sight across the Mallee: around schools, near farmhouses and in town backyards like ours. All of them incidentally, some distance from the goldfields. At the time, we valued the shade they provided and the fact that their berries made good ammunition for a bamboo pea-shooter, more than where they came from.

In the early years, the school stable was an essential building for two families who came to school by horse, one on horseback, the other in a gig. One day, Don Dundee fell out and his gig wheel ran over his stomach. He was otherwise uninjured but was the source of much amusement to recently arrived kids as, bent double, he stumbled around in circles, gasping for breath. Soon, horses gave way to bikes and lifts in parents' cars and the dividing rails of the stable, rendered smooth from years of horses scratching their flanks, remained as improvised monkey bars to swing on in the absence of playground equipment.

But we had a conventional swing. No gentle pendulum for timorous learners, this one was of a forbidding height strung between two thick unmilled posts, almost as big as those propping up the town water tanks. Only in Grade 2, I was too scared to venture onto the swing myself. Its size took on importance because Marie Conlon, a big girl for Grade 8, and always ready to defy convention, one day swung up beyond ninety degrees to the ground and fell off. She hit the ground with a sickening thud. Luckily she broke no bones, but sat, dazed and chastened, propped up with her back to the side of the school.

Between school building and stable lay the incinerator, whose presence I cannot forget. Incorrigibly brash as I was, but in this instance acting with some gravity on 1 April, I told the head teacher that someone had torn children's precious paintings from the wall of the junior room. Quite young, no act of mischief was apparently beyond me. In fact no such vandalism had occurred and I took great delight in declaring the head teacher an April Fool, much to the enjoyment of kids eagerly gathered around. Very early we learnt the pleasure of witnessing the misfortunes of others. Regrettably, I over-reached my smart potential because that afternoon, when we were all lined up ready to enter school, the same teacher asked me to go to the incinerator seventy metres down the yard. He assured me that in it he had temporarily placed a couple of stumpy-tailed lizards in a bag ready to be boxed up and sent to Melbourne University. With all eyes watching, I set off to retrieve them. I lifted the lid and, sure enough, no bag, no lizards. It was a long, slow walk back to giggling children and a smugly grinning teacher.

The only other building in the school grounds was a shelter shed with seats around the perimeter. It provided protection from all too infrequent winter rains but in summer we preferred to enjoy the breeze under the pepper tree or occasionally the kurrajong tree. A native, not an import, branches of the latter provided a vantage point to witness activity on the adjacent football field. It has pods in which seeds are embedded and surrounded by fine hairs that cause an uncomfortable itch for the curious child. Assaults from caterpillars and this: could we not have done better with our shade trees?

The footy oval had no laser-graded, mown smoothness. Rather, its surface was a mixture of bare clay down the centre and a dense covering of speargrass on the flanks. In no time, its spears penetrated our socks and began itching their passage into our ankles. On farms, it could also do terrible damage to sheep's eyes. Kurrajong and spear grass – nature sometimes has devilish ways of distributing its seeds.

I was never especially artistic; in fact, not at all. The stimulus to creativity in primary school wasn't very strong either. At Christmas time, we sat in a classroom, typically at around 100 degrees without air conditioning, earnestly making cards for our families. Mine always featured a pyramid-shaped pine tree with the obligatory star on top. Murray pines, native to our area, had branches pointing skyward not down like fir trees from the northern hemisphere which were adapted to snowfall. Not only derivative festivals but, in the wider world, writers of stories with distinctly Australian characters and settings struggled for a hearing.

The second favourite motif was a European scene: houses weighed down under a thick blanket of snow and, passing by, a team of faithful reindeer drawing a sleigh. Most kids used small packets of crayons or coloured pencils. I was a proud owner of a watercolour paint set whose tiny rectangles of colour made filling a page of painting an ambitious undertaking.

Before they departed for a life of farming, the two big Zable boys in Grade 8 spent Friday afternoons applying copper-coloured shellac to serviette rings finely turned on a lathe elsewhere. It just reduced their role from craftsmen to labourers. Maybe the Education Department had misguided beliefs of Mallee gentility because serviettes were at best an item reserved for rare visits by the local clergy. The rings were baby-skin smooth, the grain fine and the colour cream. All suggested precious Tasmanian Huon pine, trees that can last a thousand years or more, a fact not emphasised at the time. Teaching rarely involved putting objects in ecological or historical context. The smell of such French polish – shellac mixed with alcohol – remains deeply embedded in my olfactory memory. Despite its uncertain educative value, extensive rubbing at least kept the brothers out of mischief had they been inclined to mess about. Never such a risk because their dour expressions reflected a home environment of firm farm discipline. Slightly more scope for creativity – and error – was that they were allowed to use a Stanley knife to cut out bookmarks from soft, already dyed chamois leather. Again, the material just arrived from somewhere.

Happily, such faux creativity did not occupy every Friday afternoon. A special treat was the teacher's reading of Rudyard Kipling's *Jungle Book*. We sat there, for once quite still but absorbed. I'd seen Butchy Sidney's scurrying, sniffing, smelly yellow ferrets so it was not a great imaginative leap to enjoy the exploits of mongoose Rikki Tikki Tavi. Perhaps Kipling gave the cobra undue billing. Australia, after all, had its own army of ten world-ranking venomous snakes but Kipling's was a story, not a serpentology treatise. Another book titled *Nemarluk*, a tale about a tall, athletic Aboriginal warrior by Ion Idriess, met my desire for adventure and appealed to my nascent support for the underdog. Characteristically, Nemarluk died young, of illness – only twenty-nine. His white biographer went on to reach eighty nearly forty years later.

One of the better activities related to Walpeup primary school was tree-planting. Today, widespread greening of the countryside is seen as a means of softening the impact of climate change, but in these early years, the motivation seemed never to be clear. Descending the hill from the two big water towers towards the town tip was a wide median strip, ideal for putting in a few trees. Under our teacher's supervision, we delicately unwrapped the little plywood tubes to expose the magic sugar gum saplings. We planted them at regular intervals in what became known, naturally enough, as the plantation. The fact that such a species bore little relationship to the surrounding native vegetation apparently did not matter. Perpetuating or extending existing biodiversity was not yet on the horizon.

The same thinking governed the planting of sugar gums around the perimeter of the school. There were two problems. Summers were hot, desiccatingly so. Young trees need watering but for six weeks there was no ready labour force because it was our long break, the so-called Christmas holidays.

Probably driven by some nascent Protestant work ethic rather than any yet deep commitment to nature, Bruce and I set out every couple of days and walked the kilometre or so to school. We filled a bucket that we hung on a pole between us in best Asian fashion and watered these gums planted around the school ground perimeter. The bonus was an abundance of very large trapdoor spider holes on the route around the trees. Each spider covered its hole with a disc of fine web. Ignorant of their place in the local ecology, we would flick the lid off with a stick. Having poured water down the hole, we'd hold our breath as a fearsome hairy arachnid poked its legs over the lip in puzzlement at this unexpected rainstorm. Shamefully, too scared to do anything else, we had no other plan than to beat the unfortunate creature to death.

A Father Who Made It Easy

Mum's influence was most directly displayed in matters of health, food especially. Healthy food became the panacea for all ills. However, ascribing influence to a particular parent can be fraught. For me, it was shared but in very different ways. Dad's affection for us was indirect but unmistakeable, coming in actions more than words, although, on reflection, that applied to both. From earliest years, he took my interests to heart. For females, conversation is often the means of offering solace, sharing joys and developing and dissolving relationships. Even though he was a good sharer, like most males, Dad's contribution was mostly in deeds. He could tap into things important to me.

He helped me select a shanghai fork from the dwarf eucalypt Mallee scrub along the mail run. We kids knew a shanghai made for much greater accuracy than the sort of sling shot (or ginger – with a hard g – as we called it) with which David slew Goliath. Dad persuaded his friend in Melbourne of his need for something to secure heavy books and in this way obtained several thick, high-tension rubber straps. As propellants for my device, they could greatly increase the distance of any projectile and were much superior to the bicycle tubes cut in strips that other kids used. Misplaced priorities perhaps, but this weapon of mine had fearsome potential. To assess it, I one day fired an angular piece of cast iron into a sheet of galvanised iron. It penetrated it and almost passed through. I stress that I never aimed at people. Without visual confirmation, I believe I could easily land a shot among red gums on the Murray's far bank. But then, rumour has it also that big Jack Moylan, who played footy for Kiamal, could punt a bag of wheat across the river.

Besides building the yacht we sailed on a local dam, Dad

Father, age 68, 1962.

demonstrated how to embed marbles in wet plaster of Paris moulds to make shanghai shot and fishing sinkers out of melted lead from old car batteries. He arranged to borrow a truck to take us and other kids to a dam for swimming lessons – if dog-paddling can be called swimming. In return for this modest water mobility, we suffered woollen trunks that itched intolerably, provoking furtive scratching when the girls weren't watching. He encouraged our cricket, came to my football matches, monitored my gardening and together he and I built a chook house, including netting the top of it to thwart predatory hawks.

I treasured the long hours of chatting with him on the front steps as dusk closed in on the scrub to the west and the doleful onomatopoeia of a boobook owl captured the silence. Never, however, a friendly arm around the shoulder. No matter how well I played on the footy field – and at sixteen in my final year of high school, I was in the local senior team – he found it hard to praise any of my better exploits. His stance was in keeping with my giving an account of my day at high school when I got off the school bus. Success or disappointment, he would always offer the consoling 'You can only do your best.' Overt praise was not evident in other men either.

I admired Dad. Not many men in the district could speak in public with his resonance and eloquence. Not many men enjoyed conversation for its own sake and for these reasons he found his niche in a post office in a tiny community. The move from the farm could not have been better for him.

I learned later in a British military exhibition about the sort of conditions which Dad's two years in artillery forced him to endure from 1916 to 1918. I was struck by the herculean struggles for horse and man though all-engulfing mud. Then there was the gas, which earned him a small pension. I learned about these conditions only recently. The conditions they experienced came out only indirectly and then in little more than humorous anecdotes. He recalled a fellow soldier asking a French farmer's wife, 'Have you got a bit of *pain* (bread), madam?'

As we learn in books such as *The Middle Parts of Fortune* by Frederic Manning, describing the ordinary soldiers' camaraderie and their animosities in World War I France, extreme crises can be bonding experiences. Dad valued the comradeship of returned soldiers, especially at reunions. As a teetotaller, the attraction was not the supply of grog. (He did smoke until his death at nearly eighty.) With most wars, the lives of many returnees were for ever blighted by tormented dreams and alcoholism. For my father, reunions were often a source of humour. He recounted the time when Bruce went along. Straight-faced, one of the returned soldiers raised his backside off the leather chair to emit a thunderous fart. Bewildered, Bruce looked around, searching for a guide to an appropriate response until the whoopee cushion was revealed. Not one to swear either, Dad managed to enjoy life and convey to us the need for principled behaviour without moralising.

I was never privy to the disciplinary methods meted out by other Walpeup fathers but if experience at secondary school was any indication, there was some support for the axiom 'Spare the rod and spoil the child.' Dad might not have embraced us with physical affection but neither did he ever strike me in anger or simply to exert control. Not a physically imposing figure, he had authority. Imprinted on my mind is the sound of his deep voice reaching across the evening quiet to where we were kicking the footy on the vacant lot beside Simpson's store. I can see him standing erect, waiting impatiently for Bruce and me to come to the evening meal. We scurried home, heads bent like reprobate Adam and Eve cast out of the Garden of Eden on Mr Noak's coloured RI pictures. His authority was unquestioned because in all his other actions he demonstrated that he was on our side.

The Exquisite Pleasure of Murray River Fishing

When people provide enjoyable experiences, those who make them possible seem to take on some of the approval associated with them. Not that my father needed additional help, but fishing trips to the Murray River did him no harm. Before the time when, still a non-swimmer, I was considered old enough to join him, fishing trips had all the allure a young boy could wish for. Imagine my response when his catch included a seventy-three-and-a-half pound (thirty-three-kilogram) Murray cod. This was before it became illegal to extend cross lines from one river bank to the other. I stared at this spotted monster, big as a pig, lying on the kitchen table, my goggling eyes meeting its glazed and lifeless orbs. No longer would its huge semicircular mouth gulp down the shrimps and Murray crayfish on which it lived or be enticed by the mussels Dad used for bait. What depths were needed to nurture such a leviathan? I wondered

Not that fishing trips were without hazards. People taking time out for a refreshing swim had to contend with hidden snags and a deceptively strong current that brought huge risks. The threat rose by a quantum if the swimmer was drunk. No such risky behaviour from Dad or his companion. Neither he nor Fred Warren, his sometime fishing companion, was a drinker. Besides, their interest was catching fish, not trying to compete with them in their home territory. It might have been a help had one not been averse to the anaesthetising effect of an occasional whisky because somehow – probably when he was casting out – Fred securely anchored a hook to the fleshy part of his thumb. There was nothing to numb the throbbing pain as Dad cut it out and more than enough to disturb the equilibrium of the normally stoic farmer.

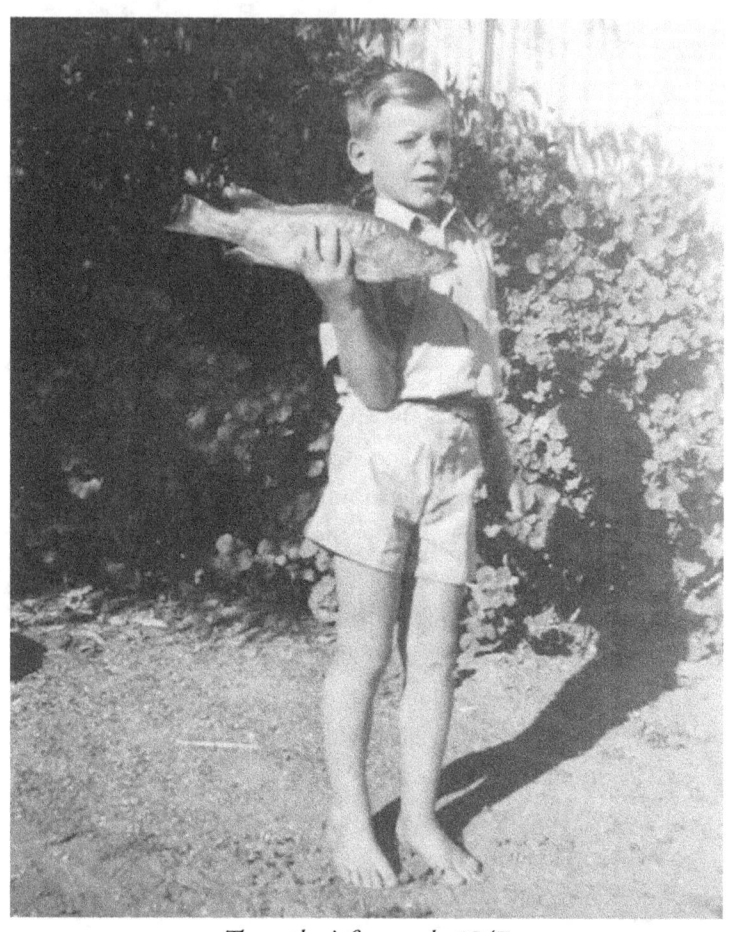

The author's first catch, 1947.

Over several weeks, I avidly watched Dad and his neighbour, another fishing companion, backs bent, cigarette dangling from lips, patiently soldering sheets of galvanised iron in our backyard to make a flat bottom boat. It was just eleven feet, three-and-a-half inches (3.4 metres) long. To provide a modicum of control in the river current, they bolted a heavy wooden keel to the bottom. When they drove to the river, with boat on trailer, they packed hessian bags of straw and later chaff on either side of the keel to double as travel stabilisers and mattresses.

We did not own a trailer ourselves for my first fishing trip but Dad, gregarious as he was, had no difficulty borrowing one. It was fashioned from an old tourer car with spoked wheels. There was no spare tyre for it so Dad and his three sons had to trust to good fortune. With its old tyres, punctures could routinely be expected over a gravel road, on a journey of no more than 110 kilometres. Because the final approach to the Murray was flat, dry clay on the flood plain, it presented no problem.

The inevitable happened halfway to our destination. Irregular tugging on the Ford V8's tow bar indicated to Dad that we indeed had a puncture in the trailer tyre. More than that, when we stopped to examine it, the tube was shredded. After a bit of head scratching and a brief sample of his usual ironic humour, Ian improvised and began stuffing the tyre with straw. He then borrowed from the neighbouring railway fence a length of number 8 wire – what some farmers say now is their saviour, their own duct tape – and with pliers twisted it around the stricken tyre. With it patched up, we climbed back in to continue the journey, dreaming of a haul of cod, yellow belly (golden perch) and grunter (Macquarie perch).

As happens with age on any vehicle, things tend to loosen a bit and parts compete with one another instead of cooperating as they are supposed to do. No question, our borrowed trailer was old. A motorist barrelling towards us in a cloud of dust unaccountably slowed down and, as he drew alongside, gesticulated wide-eyed towards our rear.

Dad checked the rear-vision mirror and shouted, 'Struth! It's alight! The trailer's burning!'

Sure enough, smoke was billowing from the left-hand trailer tyre, the one with smouldering straw. He pulled to a sudden stop and all four of us leaped out to inspect the damage. My immediate fear was that the trip might be abandoned until Ian grabbed the water container and doused the smouldering tyre. We stood a moment in a semicircle gazing at the blackening ruin then climbed back in. At frequent intervals thereafter, at the first signs of smoke, we would stop and Bruce and I became firemen, taking turns to drench the stricken tyre until satisfied there were no more wisps of smoke emerging. I was relieved to feel that I was doing something towards the continuation of the long-awaited trip.

As was Dad's custom, we called in on his old World War I mate, Len Walters, a market gardener not far from the river's bank. Even as a kid I could see that he, his wife and son Frank were struggling financially on their small irrigated property. I was puzzled by the contradiction between the bleak vision of the small property and Mr Walter's equanimity. Above all, he was hugely generous. He loaded us with cantaloupe, tomatoes or whatever else was in season. I was beginning to see that those with the least to give often give most. On this occasion, he was able also to offer us another tyre and tube to fit the trailer. Not only that, he gave us a report of where the fish were said to be biting. More than their war experience, what Dad and Mr Walker shared was a generous view of mankind and their unfailing optimism. Arguably, they unconsciously saw this trait in one another but it promoted a selflessness that could be to their detriment as Dad found in his farming days.

The next Murray River trip involved an advance in technology, a trailer with metal hub and tyre held in place by a circle of spring steel. Again, it was a borrowed one. Nevertheless, technological advance did not ensure better luck. We had another puncture and the vital spring rim catapulted into the scrub. Wilfully, it had sped off across the sand like an electronically guided hoop. Again, my immediate fear was that the trip might be shortened but it was allayed by the knowledge that we had overcome a similar challenge before. In addition, given that Mum was relieving in the post office, Dad was not tied to a tight schedule. With dusk approaching, the thin trail grew faint and we had no option but to camp and resume the search – a more successful one – at first light.

It is interesting how much privation and discomfort can be endured in the interests of recreation and pleasure. The transition from straw-filled bags to chaff-filled ones for sleeping might on the surface might have meant greater comfort but the improvement was relative. Frequently, errant bits of chaff escaped. It was difficult to know which was worse: determined chaff particles or swarms of mosquitoes. Their siren whines and liking for juvenile blood sent us into a writhing frenzy of itching. The trouble was, after a while, our imagination filled in the gaps of reality. In the absence of mosquito repellent, the buzzing, biting scourge could be thwarted with a very smoky fire but that too had its obvious drawbacks, including the need to breathe. Desperate times lead to desperate measures. Mossies don't like breeze. On one occasion, it was worth sleeping out on a sandbank to capture the gentle circulation of air even if it meant using half tyres as headrests. Some have suggested that the enjoyment of camping is like the pleasure of strenuous exercise: greatest when you stop.

Until we started catching fish, a less than luxurious diet was accepted, in the knowledge that it was temporary. We enjoyed roughing it, a nascent Robinson Crusoe sense that we would survive. We could improvise; part desire and part necessity, because writing lists was not Dad's forte. It became routine for him to ask us, well on in our journey, when return home was not a realistic option, what items we had forgotten. This time it was a can opener. Ian to the fore again. No lightly seared goat's meat nestling in a sauce of fresh cranberries, topped with a sprinkling of parmesan and coriander. With a mercifully accurate blow with our axe, Ian opened a can of Camp Pie which had the consistency and texture of Spam and was about as nutritious. This display of skill showed there was some pay-off for his miserable life on the farm.

As dawn broke and warm sun and gentle breeze dispersed mosquitoes, there was a mixture of relief and anticipated pleasure to wake to the crackling of burning eucalypt, the smell of wafting smoke, and the sound of spitting as fish fried in a pan. In the 1940s, we had kilometres of river bank to ourselves and could expect to be eating what we caught. These native fish were never muddy like carp. It was deeply satisfying to sit around the fire and chat, breakfast on a tin plate in our lap, kookaburras' final reveilles and cockatoo screeching cutting a path across river water's silent travelling. Few experiences invoke such a sense of timelessness. But then this all occurred in the enveloping protection of a father so manifestly in his element. Never an anxious person, Dad was never more serene than when he was planning the day's fishing, the spot, the bait, and the anticipated catch. He loved the Murray and according to Mum, whose preoccupation with solid brick houses was well established, Dad would have us living in a tent on the river bank if given half a chance.

From one perspective, Dad should not have got off so lightly. No child is ever privy to the inner workings of parental relationships and so it was never possible to assess whether he himself contributed to Mum's sometimes inflammatory behaviour. In never retaliating, he might have deprived her of the oxygen she desired, the sense that she mattered even if it came in disputation or anger. Whatever the reason, Dad on a fishing trip was especially good to be with.

It was our custom to row and later use the tiny 2.5-horsepower Seagull outboard motor to take us across or along the river. Ever reliable and economical and weighing only about sixteen kilograms, our motor was never going to be called on to tow waterskiers. It was our custom to tie up to a snag or tree branch projecting out of the water, preferably in the shade. As helmsman, I had a few things to learn about tying rope, such as a knot that would not come undone. Dad had good reason to once ask, 'Is this the bend where we started out?'

Once Dad had securely hooked up, we would sit there watching tiny flies skating across the water. With their long black legs, they traced mesmerising concentric circles, widening, merging and then disappearing as a zephyr of wind ruffled the surface. Bottle swallows twittered in delight as they fluttered in and out of mud homes lined up beneath the overhanging bank. Instinctively, they knew that there they were out of reach of marauding snakes and goannas. The skill, the patience of these industrious creatures as they applied the little daubs of mud to form their bottle-shaped dwellings! In flight, with grace and acrobatic agility they plucked insects from the air, inscribing as they did their place in the web of life. Black ducks, the fastest of them all, whizzed down the river and around the bend like stealth bombers. My attention shifted. I imagined down deep beneath us, cod swimming lazily, head pointing upstream, tail waving gently, in among fallen trees that break the current and offer a place to feed and breed.

It was near such snags that with a makeshift bamboo rod I caught my first fish, a 3.5-pound (1.6-kilogram) cod. Fish don't cave in without a fight and cod have their own way of resisting: a preliminary nibble then a quick resolute tug threatening to wrench the rod from my grasp. The tactile memory remains with me. I can also still see the cavernous mouth and shiny scales of my fish shimmering in the light as it veers from side to side in a last struggle at arm's-length depth in the pale green water. The water was clearer then. European carp had yet to turn this proud river into a roiling muddy drain. Dad always heightened the sense of anticipation by telling us to respond to any message coming up our lines with our own retaliatory tug. When he felt a fish jigging while he was rolling a cigarette, he always feigned annoyance, in reality delighted that they were biting!

More out of simple generosity than a desire to reward my success, Dad had ensured that Santa left me a short, flexible steel fishing rod beneath the Murray pine tree that each year we erected in the lounge room for Christmas. With the rod's strength and whip-like flexibility, I knew it would never break. Encouraged by my landing the cod on a bamboo rod, it was time to put this new equipment to the test. I walked about two hundred metres along the river to a spot where the bank was steep and a nest of snags encircled a pool. With no definitive proof, I determined it would be deep and a fish was waiting for me. It was a feeling in my core that my judgement would be vindicated, a sensation much stronger than hope. Within minutes of dropping the worm-baited line – what I learned to be choice food of yellow belly – my rod began arching feverishly. It was an unmistakeable response.

Unlike the cod with its desultory nibble then almighty tug, the yellow belly fought like a cornered wild cat. The line snaked back and forth. I quickly reeled in, fearing it would catch on one of the snags. My heart pounded with anxiety and delight. I hauled the nearly four-pound (1.8-kilogram) fish up on to the bank and, with it still dangling, headed triumphantly back to father and brother.

Searching in a lagoon for mussels, the favoured bait of cod, was both a preparation and an existential pleasure. Having felt around with our bare feet in the soft mud and gathered a sizeable quantity of mussels, we sat contentedly in the shade. On a dead half-submerged tree opposite, a jet-black shag stood motionless, its wings extended in crucifixion position to dry in the sun. Shags and ducks are both water dwellers, so why was the shag not designed so that water also ran off its back? (Lagoon, cut-off meander and billabong: interesting that so many similar things in nature were given more than one name!)

Our reverie was broken as a green and red kingfisher darted down to pluck a tiny wriggling fish and flew back into the trees. In the lagoon's centre, like a tiny north Atlantic wartime convoy, a mother duck escorted her brood of fluffy offspring, zipping in and out of the reeds behind her. More ducks, this time, fast-flying black ones, glided in from our right, spread their wings and webbed feet and dropped into the water with nary a splash. A moment later, pelicans like high-winged Sunderland flying boats glided in. Legs and wings outstretched, bodies at forty-five degrees, they landed with an audible swoosh. So much of our time at the Murray was passive, being, not doing.

There were times when fish ignored wriggling worms, treated with disdain the shrimps lured into a bucket with a putrid sheep's head, or were unimpressed by our mussels. On such occasions, we sat in boat or on bank just gazing in wonder at the elephantine limbs of 300-year-old red gums. Four metres in girth, roots reaching out to river, their taproots driven deep, six to seven metres into water-bearing aquifers below. Our thoughts were tempered in the knowledge that without warning, a limb of several tonnes could snap off and crash to the ground. Allegedly it could happen on the most windless, hot summer's day, maybe because loss of moisture made limbs brittle. Widow-makers, they called them, and a warning to campers about to pitch their tent. Sometimes, a whole tree would fall. The still air would be rent when one whose roots had been undermined by the eroding current crashed into the water with a profound rumble that rolled down the river. In response, white cockatoos screeched out from the tree they had noisily festooned like balls of cotton wool. They continued to chorus their collective annoyance long after the echo had faded.

Falling trees, bird songs and occasional plop of a fish in pursuit of an insect landing back in the water – these were nature's events: unpredictable, absorbing, but never alarming.

Induction Into the World of Adults

On the balance sheet of growing up in such a small community, there was the seeming advantage of early induction into adult life. I say seeming, because it can mean acquiring a premature seriousness. No doubt the relative dearth of children contributed. Probably the main influence was familial: even though some I saw only once or twice, we had nine elderly aunts and uncles, my mother's siblings. (Or was it eight, because I never met several?) The word sibling has rather more youthful connotations than one could fairly associate with this cohort of relations. Then for several years, my maternal grandmother lived with us. The result of all this was that Bruce and I developed something of a deference to the needs of the aged. Unfortunately, my inherent wilfulness meant it was soon overcome in the pursuit of more self-interested objectives.

Such a deference was fostered by a culture in which the transition from child to adult was swift. Adolescence had few markers, although it was not yet the time when man and child distinctions were ironed out by the universal wearing of jeans. In few areas did young people accelerate more quickly into adulthood than in the use of motor vehicles: tractors, trucks, utes and cars. I couldn't avoid it; I was up for a driving lesson.

Uncharacteristically for the age, Mum drove our car on the mail run – or, more accurately, aimed it. Most often it was she who handled the twenty-mile (thirty-two-kilometre) mail delivery while Dad worked in the post office. Wanting to set in motion this rite of passage, she determined that no age was too young to learn how to drive. When I was ten, she put me behind the wheel of our 1939 Ford V8, a vehicle that made few concessions to comfort but lacked nothing in power. The chosen site for my lesson was what Mum thought a conveniently

The author, early theatrical performer, 1943.

straight gravel strip on the mail run. (I soon gathered that learning to turn was to come in lesson two.) Overall, the road alternated between slippery muddy patches in winter, when it was a matter of skating over rather than driving through, and sand drift in summer, impenetrable without a good run-up. Her choice of a relatively firm gravel strip without bends was therefore a reasonable one. I was more nervous than excited at being about to mark an important step along life's trajectory.

Was it poor seat adjustment or were my legs short of a few inches to work the pedals? Our Ford's brake, clutch and accelerator were of the sturdy industrial type. Quivering, acting on instructions, I began to simultaneously release clutch with left foot and press accelerator with right. We crawled along in uncomfortable silence and intermittent kangaroo hops.

Mum in her gentle way yelled, 'Accelerate! Put your foot on the accelerator! Harder!'

With that, I lifted my left foot off the clutch and stretched my right leg full length. Like a start at Le Mans, we took off. I tried desperately to control the vehicle now snaking crazily from side to side, gravel pounding mudguard like buckshot. Cars at full revs at close quarters are the epitome of uncontrolled aggression and have always terrified me. Changing gears was also something to come later so, in first gear, the Ford's revs reached a scream.

Her voice risen to equal pitch, Mum shouted, ,Stop! Stop!,

Needing no further encouragement, I stretched my right leg as much as I could and rammed my foot on the brake. We skidded to a halt, the engine stalled to silence and we both sat breathing heavily. Before seat belts, Mum had already braced herself with outstretched arms; mine extended rigidly on the steering wheel. I can't remember whether I pleaded to be released from driving responsibility but I was enormously relieved to defer further instruction until later.

Under Dad's more sober tutelage, I learned to drive and, by the age of fifteen, began delivering mail and bread to several farmers down south along this same mail run. In the district, transitioning from riding a bike to driving car or truck was seen as requiring no more skill and, in most, often carried little more sense of responsibility. Underage driving was the norm. Like most boys, I was competitive, not in the drag race sort of way but against the clock. My time-keeper was the one in the post office. With bread and farmer's mail on my lap and driver window open, I'd screech to a halt beside old cream can or four-gallon drum doing service as a mailbox. I would shove supplies in and roar off, racing through the gears, determined to shave minutes off my previous time.

Morrow's hill provided a special thrill. It reminded me of a picture of the Matterhorn I saw in the *Saturday Evening Post*. A major difference was an accumulation of drift sand on the leeward side. The only option, therefore, was to charge at it in second gear. At the crest, the

Ford would hang suspended in the air in a moment of weightlessness before it dipped into hair-raising descent. Some spent good money at fairgrounds for that sort of thrill.

Ascent into the adult world had its benign aspects. Swinging an axe and shouldering dead pines in the company of adults to clear the area that became Walpeup Lake enabled a sort of maturation by osmosis. This natural depression annually took the overflow of surplus water once it had made its long, slow journey from Grampian storages in the previously mentioned Wimmera-Mallee Stock and Domestic Reticulation System. For decades, since the Mallee opened up, it had flowed sluggishly northwards in open channels laboriously excavated by horse and scoop. In many cases as water passed through sand, up to ninety per cent just soaked away or evaporated in transit.

It seemed that fifteen was to be a significant age. Another rite of passage occurred that year. What youth would pass up the chance of demonstrating his skill and strength? Chin-ups on horizontal bar; press-ups on the floor; and daily wood-chopping: my preparation had been dedicated. Dad and other local men, equipped with crowbars and shovels, were united in the task of bringing Walpeup into the twentieth century and access to mains electricity. No pushover, these pole holes along the main road from Ouyen had to penetrate clay and limestone to a depth of 1.7 metres. For several years, our lighting had been provided by a noisy, smelly generator and, before that, homework was completed by an equally toxic and stuttering kerosene lamp.

Even better than inviting myself into such company was to be given sole responsibility for something normally undertaken by adults. Fred Warren, Dad's fishing mate, asked me to be caretaker of their farm five kilometres out of Walpeup while he and family took a short holiday. It entailed an element of trust which I found flattering but garden watering was scarcely high skill and I was now a practised milker. Even so, farm management has its pitfalls. I figured that if drinking a glass of milk was good for health, then consuming a litre of it steaming straight from the cow must multiply the benefit. My bike ride home was a decidedly bilious one. Sister Fay did in fact nickname me Billious, in affection. But that epithet long preceded my experience in farm management.

My being picked for the senior Walpeup football side when I was sixteen was more a measure of shortage of players than any exceptional talent I displayed at that time. True, I was always physically fit. On one occasion, selectors decided to position me against Curly, fellow high school student from Tempy. The apparent assumption was that, like a bank robber preparing for a heist, I had made a detailed analysis of his every move at school and that this would somehow enable me to counter his extraordinary ability. He could mark a ball with absolute assurance, run with it and loft it sixty metres with disturbing ease. Curly went on to be selected twice to play interstate VFL football, the highest achievement possible. Needless to say, in that match I was kept busy.

An incident reinforced the fact that muscles as well as attitude and temperament take a while to reach maturity. In another match, an adult bank clerk from Ouyen flew above me for a mark and, on landing, his chin rammed my head down onto my shoulders. Steel jawed that he was, he didn't even sustain a cut lip! I, meanwhile, briefly unconscious then held my head, thinking, I've broken my neck! Dad was never very impulsive but could still be decisive. He immediately sped out on to the footy oval to witness my first experience of smelling salts. Into the car, we circled out of the reserve and onto the gravel road, thirty kilometres to Ouyen hospital.

By this stage, Dad had lashed out, somewhat to Mum's disapproval, and bought a sleek, second-hand navy blue 1948 Dodge. The purchase did have a tinge of recklessness but I figured he deserved a bit of luxury. Especially gratifying to me was that our new vehicle had delightfully soft springing and as we headed for Ouyen hospital at an exhilarating 110 kilometres an hour, we barely touched the road. It was the closest thing to what I imagined flying to be. Watching the scrub whizz by, I forgot my fears of paraplegia.

For the next five days, I sat in hospital bored mindless with a brace around my neck. Today, it would be simply a matter of an X-ray, a pat on the back, and off home, but still with a brace. If my treatment was a little on the cautious side, we at least had access to a hospital, doctor and nursing staff, privileges not always shared by people in small country towns.

The social significance of Saturday football and netball cannot be overemphasised. In my early childhood, the footy league consisted of Ouyen, Kiamal, Tiega and Walpeup. It expanded to include Tempy, Patchewallock and Gorya. (Unearthing the origins of such team names is a ready-made challenge for any budding local historian.) In my time, during a match in the recreation reserve, cars faced inwards, to form an unbroken ring around the ground. Only in extreme cold or rare heavy rain would spectators stay in their vehicles and toot a chorus of approval when a goal was scored. Mostly, men gathered behind the goals at the top end to chat and, defying creaking joints and inelastic tendons, attempt to mark the ball as it sailed between goalposts. Some women stood with them but generally, from the sidelines, cheered their daughters playing netball on an adjacent court. Others, protected from wind and rain in a rough galvanised-iron shelter, kept up a continuous supply of hot dogs. Barracking uses a lot of calories.

Not Friendless, but...

Despite the pleasure of Saturday sport, I had an unfulfilled desire for friendship. Somehow, sitting on the disused bank steps of a Sunday morning with Lacey reading *Blackhawk* comics, when not even a dog bark broke the silence, didn't fill the void. I'm not even sure that I behaved honourably towards the young people with whom I might have been friends – my behaviour towards Lacey, for example.

After that very rewarding day catching several redfin in the dam out north, my friendship with him was sorely tested – literally. With my back still covered in monstrous blisters from the afternoon's fishing, I was about to get off the bus when he whacked me on this weeping moonscape of pain for fun. The needling pain was excruciating. Overcome with indignation and confusion, I was incapable of resolving the issue there and then.

A couple of days later, in part fuelled by my residual anger, we began scuffling on the concrete outside a classroom. In the contest, I dislodged his feet. Not to be denied, now lying on his back, he locked both legs around me in what he thought to be a decisive manoeuvre: the Boston crab, he hissed triumphantly. I wasn't especially interested in the manoeuvre's pedigree. My immediate need was to reduce the extreme pressure around my midriff and resume breathing. I stiffened my thighs, lifted his whole body up and dumped him. He gasped and his legs fell away. Concussion? Severed spinal cord? I shudder to think of what might have been the outcome for him but fortunately for me he just emerged with damaged pride. Certainly not one of my most glorious moments.

What about the Cosgrove family who lived up near Mr Pit's rambling workshop and where Mr Cosgrove once worked before business dried up? Did an unconscious disapproval of their poverty, their indifference to cleanliness, or their lack of interest in schooling block any lasting friendship with them? My sense of superiority didn't preclude an occasional willingness to exploit them, especially to enhance my collection of birds' eggs. Their son Reggie's short muscular frame and biddable nature made him ideal to send up trees that I would never dare to climb. The idea was that he would descend with an egg for me in his mouth. His reward was to be an egg too but spitting noises and a stream of yolk from aloft told me he wasn't always going to get his cut of the takings.

I had no solid friends in town. I maintained it did not reflect any objectionable personal habits; there were simply few kids of my age and, possibly, temperament. OK, I did enjoy the Sunday-morning reading of comics with Lacey, even if the draw was mainly the comics themselves. He was also co-researcher in my smoking experiments – anything that permitted the inhalation of air and smoke. What came through lengths of an old cane pram and the fine roots of young Mallee trees might have been uncomfortably hot but they were infinitely cheaper and more available than Monopole Midget cigars that we smoked in the dunny outside the Methodist church.

The one who should have cemented himself as a friend was David Brown but the lack of warmth in our relationship led me to realise that we were no more than two people in the same place with a common chore. Simply thrown together. Almost daily, he and I scoured the fringes of town on bikes looking for the cow that each of our families possessed. Several things worked against possibilities of friendship. First was the fact that he was younger than I was. He was a Catholic and, even though my claims to Presbyterianism were shaky at best, there was an ineradicable subterranean suspicion of Catholics among Protestants. In a culture where sport was king, he demonstrated superior football skills. Proof of this, he was later recruited into the elite Victorian Football League. In country towns, sporting prowess topped everything. To heap indignity on humiliation, he soundly beat me in a two-person bike race in front of a local crowd at a Walpeup carnival. To make things even worse, I feared he might have been doing better at school than I was. Jealousy is a hard nut to crack. For all his undoubted achievements, or because of them, we never became close friends.

I was tied to the relationship with David by dint of our needing to graze our cows, and it lasted several years. I couldn't forget it. However, it is amazing how recollections of events that are short-lived and embarrassing can be readily suppressed. I was persuaded, or shamed, into taking a ride on Butchy Sidney's horse. I mounted the wretched beast up the hill near the primary school and it set off at what it seemed to regard as a respectful trot. I pulled on the reins. I pulled harder but it was clear the horse would not be halted. Every time my backside rose up from the saddle, I was overcome with panic and feelings of powerlessness. An interminable fifteen minutes later, it stopped near the main street. Was it all part of the horse's plan? I wondered.

A semblance of pride returned when Ashton's Ccircus came to town. Undaunted by my previous experience – or rather, perceiving the odds to be more in my favour – I accepted the challenge as a boy under eleven to ride a Shetland pony. Just once around the ring was expected. By that stage, I had begun to grow, was heavy for my age, and the animal sagged under my weight. It staggered the circuit and at the end I collected my shilling. Just reward, I thought, for previous ignominy.

Given the dearth of friends in town, I was more than attentive when Mrs Coleman began talking with Mum on a Saturday morning. Mum's friend – seemingly her only one – was the mother of twin boys almost exactly my age. Shopping finished, mothers' brief exchange over, a stay at their farm was in the offing. After an excited packing, all four of us piled into the back of their ute and, with wind parting our hair and their dogs' saliva lashing our faces, we tore along the sandy bush track to their farm. The twins left school just before turning fourteen, the legal age for quitting. By that stage, they knew both the language and practice of farming in detail and saw little reward in continuing a schooling that met almost none of the needs of prospective farmers. Preparation for succession began at an early age and the twins already had an income and surely a bank account.

Mrs Coleman's husband Clarrie was a phlegmatic English World War I veteran. Like Dad, he had a spoil of war – a Turkish belt that he clipped around his ample stomach covered in a grey short-sleeved flannel item that doubled as singlet and shirt. Always a man of few words, one day while we all sat respectfully ready to eat the dinner that his wife prepared, he spotted a fly crossing the table. It had the temerity to ignore the sticky flypaper dangling from the ceiling in search of something sweet below. In the Coleman household, once one of the boys had uttered the obligatory 'For what we are about to receive, may the Lord make us truly thankful' with machine-gun rapidity, there seemed to be an unwritten rule that the meal table was not for conversation. Silence imposed a discipline I had yet to acquire. Suddenly, with an unnerving thud, Clarrie lunged and brought a knife blade down on the table to sever the errant fly in two. The shock probably did more to shorten our lives than any bacteria the now dissected fly might have spread.

As usually happens, one partner is left with the task of communication and maintenance of domestic harmony, and typically, it was the woman. Mrs Coleman cheerfully cared for her twin sons and, before that, two older boys who by then had left home. When the culture offered no alternative, many women revealed no discontent with their lot – at least in the eyes of young children. They drew comfort in the completion of tasks they were allotted. While she slaved away in a primitive outdoor washhouse, money always seemed to be available for the latest in tractor, header or combine. Yet had the issue been raised, Clarrie might have said that these machines provided household income.

Whatever other virtues Mrs Coleman had, one endeared her to me. She baked Anzac oatmeal biscuits, rich in golden syrup, and melting moments, sweet, disc-shaped biscuits held together with an even more sugary substance. I appreciated that she knew we needed something to get us through several hours' privations in a cubby or bush hut out in the scrub.

Mrs Coleman was a woman of the Mallee. Their realm was the domestic one and the pinnacle of long experience cooking for Country Women's Association (CWA) fund-raising stalls was to submit their proud creations to the Royal Agricultural Show in Melbourne. Activities extended beyond the act of baking fruit cakes and sponge cakes. Great dedication and artistry went into crafts and cake decorations featuring flower arrangements, farm and nativity scenes, and fairy tales. Surely they were no more ephemeral than a theatrical performance and just as worthy a testament to human creativity. Once winners were announced, women would walk past discreetly numbered cakes and bottled fruit and vegetables arrayed on trestles. Some lingered with quiet satisfaction, others pursed their lips in disappointment. Unwritten rules forbade extravagant display of emotion. That would be unseemly.

Hot dry summers led to another innovation on many farms: the cellar. In principle, it made use of the earth's insulation potential while ensuring protection from the sun. Thus, above a large rectangular excavation, farmers built a sloping roof of thatching or galvanised iron but covered with a deep layer of the excavated soil and stone. These refuges afforded blessed relief in temperatures much below those outside. For the Colemans', it was also the storage space for jars of a variety of fruit and vegetables grown in the garden which Mrs Coleman tended. Each was cooked in the Fowlers tub and kept airtight with spring clips. They sat on shelves cut into the sides of the cellar, along with bottles of home-brewed ginger beer. Occasionally, gas built up inside the ginger beer and a bottle would explode, sending a cascade of glass and sugary liquid over its fellow preserves. Undeterred by any such unscheduled detonation, we even lunched in the cellar's welcome coolness, enjoying a sort of underground picnic.

Only three when my family left our family farm, I nevertheless heard the story of our own cellar. Mum and Dad had taken to sleeping in it to escape summer heat. But a large brown snake had the same idea and it was somewhat restless. Mum avers that in darkness, it crawled slowly over her stomach while she remained rigid and petrified. The reptile made the mistake of hanging around long enough for Dad to get his shotgun and blow its head off while Mum held a torch. Even though snakes were allies in the war on mice, ecological understanding was yet to emerge and to that point they were the enemy.

One quality I had some difficulty in accepting was Mrs Coleman's insistence that when tree leaves hung listlessly and even cicadas felt summer's heat too much, the boys and I should have a post-prandial nap. Spaniards and people in their dotage might have felt it necessary but I didn't. Rather than sleep – and I never saw the value of resting – I would lie obediently, listening to the noise of the wireless coming through the thin lath and plaster wall of their old farmhouse.

'Yes, Agnes, Mary tells me that Shirley is expecting in August. She's sure it is going to be a boy. Our Dottie had a girl and I said to her, I said to her, never mind. She'll be a good helpmate.' After similar riveting exchanges, the rising strings of theme music rounded out yet another insight into rural life followed by 'And so ends episode 347 of *Blue Hills* by Gwen Meredith.' This ABC saga of rural life began in 1949 when I was in Sixth Grade and continued for the next twenty-seven years to rack up eye-glazing numbers of episodes. Like all theatre, it reflected a life back to the audience which they could enjoy without penalty.

Throughout the 1940s and I still under ten, it was acceptable and expected that I would spend weekends and holidays at play. Sometimes, as with building cubbies in the bush with the Coleman twins, it involved making use of what nature provided. Another natural feature at that time was huge sandhills up to thirty or forty feet (twelve metres) high. Wind and soil desiccated by high temperatures and low rainfall were the malignant army, the aggressive culprits for this destructive accumulation of sand. The unwitting soldiers – both real and metaphorical – behind the lines were fallible human beings whose knowledge of land management did not match the environmental challenges. Having already removed most of the soil-holding tree cover, in their desire to eke out a living, they over-cultivated.

By the early 1940s, the Mallee Research Station at Walpeup attracted many farmers to its field days, keen to learn about new wheat varieties and how to combat yield destroying flag and ball smut and rust. A message hard to convey was that the soil must be protected as the source of wealth. It did not help that those of the 8,600 World War I soldier settler farmers allocated land in Victoria who were engaged in dry farming, had only rudimentary knowledge. In addition, their blocks were too small for prevailing environmental and economic conditions. The temptation to mine the land was therefore strong and as a consequence sand piled up against scrub and fences, anything likely to resist wind's onward march.

Sand not only accumulated in hills. Roads between farms were little more than winding, sandy tracks requiring focus by any motorist not wishing to be wrapped around bordering trees. (In fact, when steering gave way on our Erskine, this happened, and as an infant on Mum's knee, I allegedly received a small piece of glass above my right eye. Carrying infants on one's knee was far from being the only unsafe motoring practice.)

In the 1940s and 1950s, Mallee wheat and sheep farms were a third or quarter the size of properties today. This meant that houses were closer together, within walking distance. On one memorable expedition with the twins, Bruce and I set our minds on a very large sandhill anchored on a long-submerged fence near a neighbouring farm. Foolishly, to get to our destination, we removed our shoes too early so that we had to scamper across the burning sand crystals from the shade of one tree to the next like Pacific Island fire-walkers or desert geckos. What followed was massive fun. For over an hour, we staggered breathlessly up the slope of the highest hill, momentarily took in the view, and hurled ourselves forward like roly polys, head over heels to the bottom. Adrenalin surging but undaunted by the climb, we again lurched into the challenge and, once more pausing to glance over the countryside, launched out in giant uncontrolled strides to the bottom.

The farm nearest the hill was still a functioning one but they only had two girls, and playing with the opposite sex was still foreign territory.

With twins Jim and Neville Coleman, chores were good fun too, but gathering chook eggs was no simple task, basically a form of ongoing strategic warfare, akin to narcotics agencies trying to keep ahead of drug-cheating athletes. By day, the hens roamed free and exercised their right to lay anywhere: in the haystack, in the barn, in the stable, or in the old smithy (blacksmith premises) and yes, occasionally in the chook house. It required a modicum of courage to reach under a clucky hen sitting on a clutch of eggs, only too ready to defend her setting with sharp pecks. It remained an early lesson to me of the strength of maternal instinct.

For further recreation, the four of us helped yard sheep. Essentially, we were spectators because, with minimal backward glance, at Clarrie's whistle or 'Go way back', the two kelpie sheepdogs could circle, stop, dart forward, yelp and turn the seemingly brainless sheep to the pens for shearing or crutching. Once in the sheep yard, they would jump up, run along the sheep's backs like an ant up a tree, reinforcing their control with barking in the ears of the leading animals. No wonder that a farmer's saddest day was when, with a bullet to the temple, he had to bring to an end the life of a dying kelpie.

At other times, we were more active. We pointlessly trampled wool in the baler while father Clarrie displayed a furtive smile. We plundered dozens of sparrow nests in the thatched hay roofs of old sheds. We heaved up and down on the end of the enormous bellows in their old smithy surrounded by numerous bits of iron discarded in the process or running repairs on farm machinery. Most enjoyable of all was to harness the sole horse to a cart, load a bundle of rabbit traps and set out on a jogging, horse-farting journey along sandy tracks to areas still blighted by rabbit warrens.

In quieter moments, we gazed enviously on the twins' older brother's collection of birds' eggs and were in awe of his bow and arrow hanging on the wall. It was like peering into the secret life of a backwoodsman.

There was one disturbing element in my relationship with these two boys, who left school quite young, as I said, already farmers with an income and keen to go full time. We attended their Christmas concert in their primary school deep in the Mallee scrub. My overriding feeling was that their school's rendition of 'Kookaburra Sits in the Old Gum Tree' was amateurish, the pictures of wildlife, nativity scenes and drawings of family and decorations adorning the walls unsophisticated, and the ensemble of activities cringe-worthy. I said nothing of my feelings to them both out of learned politeness and a dim awareness that their life was deservedly of more interest to me than mine was to them anyway. Disturbingly, I have no idea where my shameful condescension came from. In my schooling to that point, there seemed to be no obligation to engage in invidious comparison and implicit defence of what I had been exposed to in Walpeup. Egalitarian the culture of our town might have been, but such disturbing reactions are cause to reflect. Simpler causes might have been in play. A child brought up by a micro-managing mother is likely to be both severely self-critical and critical of others.

Farmer Speech Patterns and Behaviour

My life in Walpeup consisted of a fluctuating combination of obligation, routine and the search for fun and novelty. Sounds of many birds I could identify but, for the most part, my ear was not attuned to speech patterns around town. There were some obvious ones, including clipped Scottish Mr Pit and deep-voiced Dave Rowan. Typically, we used idioms common across the continent. Often their origins were lost in time but others were grounded in rural life. 'Stone the crows' and 'as the crow flies' (a straight line on paper) obviously paid homage to the ubiquitous big, black crows (correctly, ravens).

Metaphorical expressions added colour to life and status to the speaker and at the same time were a restricted linguistic code that cemented rural relationships. Some, such as 'pull your finger out', seemed to echo the equally derogatory expression, 'sitting there with your thumb in your bum and your mind in neutral', by way of criticism of a failure to act when the situation demanded.

Bodily functions readily found their crude language equivalents among some boys. The abundance of words available for the body's different parts also varied greatly, males' dangly bits for example.

Much of the swearing, no matter how universally indulged in, was rather innocuous by today's standards. 'Bloody', of disputed origin but often reference to Our Lady, was universal and had to be sprinkled throughout one's speech, sometimes to hyphenate words. 'Don't you under-bloody-stand?' It wasn't until mid-high school years, when a man was alleged to have had unnatural relations with a horse in a hotel yard that I learned the meaning of the other commonly used expression of frustration, 'bugger', and the harsher insult, 'go to buggery'.

There seemed to be an endless supply of Pat, Mick and Mustard stories circulating and frequently involving excretory behaviour, decidedly for a boy audience and, in retrospect, despite their designation as dirty yarns, quite benign. Short rhyming poems filled the same space except that, as in those beginning, 'There was a young lad from Horsham…' and 'The boy stood on the burning deck…', they featured real or potential threat to boys' testicles.

Not all Walpeup residents swore. Mallee language reflected gender: women and girls seemed not to swear. To a degree, language also followed religiosity, education, job and simple family background. Dad was by no means religious and uttering his strongest oath, 'blast' or 'this blasted cold', he would give voice to a minor ailment while ignoring his heart trouble and the effects of being gassed in the war. Tertiary-educated officers at the Mallee Research farm seemed to have a better grasp of our language and were less likely, I realised, to resort to cliché.

There was nothing more idiosyncratic than the speech of Jack Smythe, a good-natured bachelor farmer from somewhere out north. Having unloaded bags of wheat from the back of his creaking Ford, he was primed for conversation. He would listen attentively to what another was saying with apparently infinite capacity for amazement. 'Well,' he would begin his astonishment with an elongation of the sound and cross between 'wairl' and 'wherrrrl' and then, 'Well now! Go on! You don't say! Well I never! Good gawd!' all uttered with absolute deliberation and riveted attention. These would be repeated several times until there was no doubt that Jack was singularly impressed by this new bit of information. However, he never swore. One could speculate that had he a partner, some of his speech mannerisms might have been ironed out, but then, wouldn't that have been a pity! His desire to extract the maximum from a speech encounter doubtless reflected a degree of loneliness, something by no means confined to him.

Jack Hennessy, also a farmer, never stood still. As if to expedite his movements, he always wore tennis shoes without socks not bought purposely for work because he did play tennis. He always seemed to be bent, in readiness, like a chimp about to pounce and settle a dispute. In serving a tennis ball, he contorted his body in a helix, dissipating rather than increasing the force in the process but it must have been hugely distracting to his opponent. Everything he did was on the run and, reputedly, he expected a farmhand to move with equal alacrity. Even his driving suggested a thwarted desire to be in charge of an ambulance or fire truck. Wheat dust can be troublesome. Once, with me in the cabin of his truck, he did what was commonly called a drawback to bring the mucus and wheat dust out of his nasal passages into his mouth in readiness. Characteristically, he turned and let fly out the window. Unfortunately, he had forgotten to wind it down.

Budding Entrepreneur

Until 1955, without mains electricity and having only a manual exchange telephone, Walpeup was no seventeenth-century Amsterdam, no bustling twentieth-century Wall Street. Its chances of becoming the hub of global capitalism were always slim. Yet there were opportunities, niches they call them, for the budding youthful entrepreneur.

A source of income ultimately provided for thousands across Australia was the scourge of European wild rabbits, first introduced in 1859 near Winchelsea for the sport of gentry. Trapper Dave Rowan was not the only one who benefited from their abundance, but for landowners they were another story. Until decimated by the virus myxomatosis, rabbits would scuttle from their burrows, surging like a marauding army on early morning and evening raids to reduce a farmer's crop and income to nothing. Rabbits breed quickly – well, like rabbits. One pair can become 100 rabbits in a year. All attempts to control them, much less eradicate them, were to no avail. They were shot, poisoned, gassed, crushed in their burrows and, experimentally, even infected with cholera. The lure of bounties proved fruitless, but for me, up with the sparrows, hands freezing on the handlebars, dangling traps rattling, rabbit skins brought pocket money and the carcass delicious rabbit stew. I witnessed the devastation they could inflict. This image lessened the discomfort I felt at a trapped animal's squealing in agony and terror when caught in one of my traps. The unnerving sound travelled hundreds of metres through still, frosty air. The damage they caused helped me numb myself as I snapped the animal's neck. If any further justification for my activities were needed, their skins were used to make the Akubra felt hat that Dad and most men wore. Then came myxo and the pitiful sight of stricken animals blinded or disfigured with tumours, stumbling through their last week or two. While a godsend to farmers, the arrival of the virus meant I had to search for another source of income.

Fortunately, I had a close association with the postmaster. For every telegram delivered, Bruce and I legitimately earned sixpence, drawn apparently from Her Majesty's coffers. With this incentive, we took a keen interest in any budding romance in the district that could potentially lead to nuptial bliss. Our economic salvation lay in the wedding ceremony. When a couple committed themselves in matrimony, it was customary for people to send well-wishes to bride and groom, messages in telegrams read out at the ceremony by the best man. We were paid for each item rather than the number of trips. Energised by the bonanza of multiple sixpences, we sometimes paused to catch the ribald comments levelled at the hapless groom by his friend, who in his speech showed he was privy to his more embarrassing past behaviours. Weddings aside, at other times it was a pleasure to be the bearer of other good tidings, to folk whose beloved had trusted their lives on the train to Melbourne. 'Arrived safely. Love, Agnes.' Anything could happen to a passenger submitting to the perils of train travel: E. coli from eating a warmed-up pie on Ouyen station for a start.

Living in a remote rural community meant being influenced by the swings and roundabouts of an unpredictable climate and scourges like rabbits. But there were also opportunities to share in better economic times. In the early 1950s, triggered by post-war recovery, the Korean War and the stimulus of expanding migration, wool prices rose up to one pound a pound for quality merino fleece. Reasonably, I could only be said to be dealing with the fringes of the industry because a lucrative source of income for me was dead wool, the fibrous remains of a once noble animal, often dying along a fence and whose flesh had already provided sustenance for crows. The bodily organs and flesh might have been scavenged but the crows were not fussed about leaving the smell behind, something I ignored with the prospect of handsome financial return. I needed no more evidence that I too was part of the rural economy than to receive a handsome cheque and confirmation of my labours with Goldsborough Mort letterhead.

Beer was clearly the beverage of choice and country towns provided a reasonably secure supply of empty bottles to supplement any kid's pocket money. They brought a penny each to us and employment for the truck driver who collected them. Even if the sight of a growing stack of empties gave me a warm glow, locating the favourite Saturday-night drinking spots had some of the anticipatory pleasure of finding new chook nesting spots on Coleman's farm. However, it did not take great insight to realise that the scrub near the hall where musicians and friends nipped out for refreshment was one of the most reliable places. Regrettably, as non-drinkers, my parents were of no help in this money-making venture.

Influenced by Dad, I took a liking to gardening. Early, I learnt some things, including that too much cow manure made carrots fork and look ugly. At other times, enthusiasm took over. Very young, I loved planting broad bean seeds then digging them up to see how much they had grown. Unearthing all things hiding their gifts under the soil provided the most reward. Bean seeds first and later potatoes and carrots, digging these brought the unexpected, like finding bush mushrooms after rain, catching fish, or searching for those coins from Bertie Corbett's house fire among ashes at the local tip. All brought an element of surprise. I could understand the lure of gambling.

Soon the financial potential of tilling the soil dawned on me. In a hot, dry Mediterranean-type climate, cucumbers were easy to grow and, as a consequence, I was convinced that everyone had an insatiable desire for them, especially mine. It did not occur to me that, if they were easy to grow, others might have the same idea. I rasped indentations in the sides of a shallow box for hand grip and set forth down the street with six of my prized vegetables in anticipation of making a killing with neighbours. I sold one – to Mrs McCurdy. I had yet to learn the lesson that one should never compromise friendship with commerce.

The climatic classification under which Walpeup existed should have led us to expect cool, wet winters and hot, dry summers. Rainfall records suggested the wet winters were more promise than reality. Whatever, these elements smiled cheerfully on a particular species of cold-blooded reptile, a lizard that loved the hot sun. To their detriment, their cumbersome movements did little for their self-preservation. The lizard in question we called the stumpy-tail but shingle-back was a less common name given to it. As the names imply, it had a short tail, large triangular head and body encased in shingles. Long before there were qualms about experimentation on animals, the Zoology Department at Melbourne University paid us handsomely for any stumpy-tails we could box up and send to them. Whether the lure of money overcame any nascent distaste for vivisection or we were kept in ignorance, I don't know, but we continued while the demand was there. I had a particular advantage because not only were these omnivorous creatures slow-moving, they were common along the ten-mile route over which we delivered mail and bread every Saturday. Still in primary school, I had to rely on the driver, my mother, to collect them. It must have been a labour of love because she hated the task. Certainly, they could be nasty little buggers, hissing mouth wide open when threatened and, given the chance, biting with bacteria-encrusted teeth. Instead of grasping them behind the head in the accepted manner, Mum would lasso them with a noose in a hay band like an experienced snake catcher and drop them into a sugar bag. She tied it at the top with another hay band and with great relief thrust it into the car boot.

Unlike the contemporary US, where every day about ninety people die at the end of a firearm, locals around Walpeup directed their guns at non-human species: rabbits, foxes and ducks especially. Most farmers had a shotgun and, although Dad no longer tilled the soil, he had a double-barrelled one, the most common type. Occasionally, I went with him on the mail run to shoot a rabbit or two, although the closest I got to handling the weapon was the strict instruction to always poke it unloaded through the fence first.

Early in my journeying out with wheat carters, before I was old enough to be of any help, I was witness to the fearsome potential of a .303 rifle, the standard infantry weapon of both wars. Particularly on land near Sunset country at the edge of settlement where we were, emus could have a destructive impact on crop lands. They could eat or trample standing crops, eat bagged grain and damage fences. That was Wally Ritchie's excuse anyway. A load of wheat on board, we stopped on a rise and, far away, could see a mob of emus. His rifle sight told him they were 1,800 yards (1,646 metres) distant – over a mile. He loaded, rested the rifle on the open truck door and began firing. The echoing, unseen path of the first bullet sent galahs aloft in the depths of the scrub. A second's fraction and an emu began stumbling, kicking and eventually falling. We drove down the hill and climbed through the fence, and he killed the creature with a jack handle. A .303 bullet was reputed to carry three miles. This was totally new to me: its power and magical ability to transcend time and space and destroy life. Although never wantonly cruel, humane treatment of native creatures was not yet something I thought deeply about.

Hares and rabbits were something different. As a teenager, I borrowed a .22 (.56-centimetre) rifle with the aim of killing a rabbit in the scrub north of town where I had hopes of seeing one sitting by numerous burrows. Of the two species, the hare is the faster. It can run up to forty-five miles per hour (about seventy kilometres per hour). Not only speedy in full flight, its strong back legs afford rapid acceleration. As I passed by bushes close to the ground, one darted out and before it had travelled ten metres, I wheeled round, raised the rifle and fired. It dropped dead on the spot. I don't think it was fright. Had it been no more than wounded, I was too shocked to have pursued it.

Dad had often spoken of a dish called jugged hare, the preparation for which allegedly involved burying the carcass for a period in the ground until fermentation set in. I suspect this story expressed an aversion, widely shared, for a whole animal – according to the recipe – being slow-cooked in its own blood. I decided on the less adventurous option of asking Mum to make a normal stew using hare portions.

These two shooting incidents brought an unconscious realisation that a firearm had great appeal to those crippled by their own sense of powerlessness. I lacked the means to possess a rifle but had a still developing sense of self, sufficient not to be seduced by it.

I did play an important role in the recreational sport of others. Clay pigeon shooting was popular. The target had no resemblance to a bird but was a black, saucer-shaped disc, twelve centimetres in diameter, that readily shattered on impact. My job was to sit in a small dugout, well-protected from any misfired weapon, to operate the trap that propelled the target above the downward slope of the golf-course. When the shooter yelled 'Pull!' I could determine the point on the arc that the disc emerged by its placement on the trap arm. The shooter's aim was to be adaptable and hit the target wherever it emerged. My aim was to try to trick them, although it was not part of my job description. Artie Henneberg had what was called an 'under and over' with two barrels, one on top of the other, and that alone was not what made him special. A gun shooter, he could routinely shatter ninety-seven birds for every 100 released, no matter how much I mixed up the trajectory. Although I was not supposed to hear the shooter's name, when Dad's was called, birds somehow took a more predictable flight.

For a period, shooters targeted live pigeons. My job was to load one of the unfortunate creatures in each of five boxes. All five were connected to long wires whose handles I could release when again, the shooter yelled 'Pull!' Importantly, I was standing behind the shooter. Once a bird met its demise, and the shooter gave the all clear, I had to take another out of a crate, run down the golf course slope to fill the now vacant box, and collect the dead bird. While I had yet to develop an empathy for the unfortunate creatures, I had a sneaking admiration for the occasional one fleeing across the sky to freedom. I was aware that, to an extent, with pigeons of both the live and manufactured variety, the shooter's success lay in my hands. Animal rights weren't on the horizon. Seeming indifference to the plight of these birds alongside respect for the multitude of native topknots (crested) and bronze-wing pigeons in the wild was just one of the many contradictions of my childhood. Given that it took longer to breed a living, breathing bird, than pressing out another clay disc, this activity did not last as long and the golf course returned to its more sedentary activity. I'm sure cessation of live bird kills was not driven by humane considerations.

Given this short history of successful entrepreneurial activity, it is puzzling that as an adult, the world of business held no appeal for me whatsoever.

Girls

Until the stirrings of adolescent hormones made themselves present, my interest in girls was, frankly, zero. During the maypole dance at the birthday party of our primary teacher's daughter (Bruce, Fay and I never had a birthday party), I made the discovery that girls had softer hands than we did. I soon realised they inhabited different worlds. They didn't ride wheat trucks, they dressed differently, they played netball and not footy, and they swore less, if at all. I could not deny that some of them were bright, brighter than I was. Was it just diligence? High percentages on folded foolscap exam papers returned to us at higher elementary school, were undoubted evidence of something.

Things began to change at secondary level in other ways. The end of year social meant that boys could legitimately work alongside girls to set up the double classroom. They could liberate their creative elements with chalk drawings on the blackboard, string streamers, and devise character descriptions or, more accurately, character assassinations, for pass the parcel. Whatever the party game's origins, it was a great way to legitimately advertise the alleged failings of others and hide erstwhile secret desires beneath social play. Growing up, there is nothing worse than being ignored, so that being handed a parcel after some disparaging description had been read out was not all bad.

Socials were one time too when girls could legitimately wear fashionable hairstyles, apply lipstick and wear perfume with all its seductive overtones. What is more, it was OK to put your arm around them in the progressive barn dance. Gratefully, sometimes, their footwork wasn't much better than boys'. To be fair, many had already learned to indulge boys' clumsiness.

Things could happen away from the combined classrooms where

the social was held. As a thirteen-year-old, I was emboldened to sit with Betsy among the shrubbery in the moonlight, she with her girlfriend and I with another boy, a sort of companion of convenience for each of us to make up the numbers. Beyond nervous giggles and anxious laughter, nothing happened but it meant that from now on, as we lined up in the quadrangle, there was a tiny chink in the gender divide.

Gradually, with the lure of employment, instant income and an adult status not achievable at school, class numbers dwindled and talking with those girls left in class was inescapable. Most likely undeserved, by Fourth Form, Sylvia was identified as the Town Bike by a couple of the Ouyen blokes. They claimed to have inside information but no direct experience to assess the validity of the title. When seated in front, she also endured some bra flicking, but with feigned annoyance. The fact that she seemed to enjoy being the centre of attention hardly justified my inaction, passively not participating or not intervening. Shy and ignorant in the matter of the sexes, I was unsure whether this was the right way to treat a girl and I offered no protest.

In the schoolyard, girls had a designated area where they played vigoro, a hybrid of tennis and cricket invented in 1901. The bat was a funny-looking long-handled paddle with a thick wooden blade, the ball smaller and softer than a cricket ball. When enjoying recess-time kick to kick (or, as it was called, kickety kick), our football rolling into the girls' territory afforded a brief chance to interact. The best vigoro players also tended to have eyes for the best footballers, so that put me behind the eight ball (to coin a phrase from a game I never played). In the final years, a de facto gender equality emerged. Lack of students meant girls teamed up with us boys to play a friendly lunchtime game of tennis on the school's gypsum courts.

Tennis aside, the jury is out on whether our co-ed schooling encouraged a capacity to relate to girls as equals. For boys like me, movement to music was fun and demonstrated that girls in senior forms had a better sense of rhythm than we did. This is in spite of the fact that I was getting occasional out of school practice at our local dances. To make up the shortage of willing men on the Saturday-night dance floor in the Walpeup hall, women generously led both young boys and girls around the floor. I found a succession of entrancing perfumes a welcome change from the smells of beer, cigarettes, sweat and Brylcreem wafting around among the men at the hall entrance. Not surprisingly, in the dance halls of Ouyen, Tempy and Patchewallock, girls had long joined in the dances.

Discussions in class often seemed to be skewed towards boys who felt entitled to offer their opinion, well-founded or not. Even if boys had nothing worthy to contribute, they could still disrupt the class to get attention and, in this, I played my part. Brendan went one step further. When he began audibly slapping his erect member with a ruler under the desk, Miss Walton, petite music teacher, blushed her awareness of what he was doing but seemed powerless to confront the sniggers spreading through the class. Emphatically not a time to begin sex education.

Any sex education we got never came from practice. Lacey and I found a cache of old copies of *Man Junior* of most interest to us for its display of scantily clad women in provocative poses. There was nothing junior about them, much to our appreciation, but the title seemed designed to widen the market. It was a bit like appealing to young smokers so that readers would move onto *Man* magazine itself. As far as I could see from the one or two abandoned copies, it did not differ in the essentials. Perhaps fearing that others might come upon our find, we put them in a box up a pine tree for later access. Perusing these magazines did little more than reinforce the view of women as sex objects. They were about as helpful for forming a good understanding of the opposite sex as a publication called *Father and Son* that Ian bought for us. Early teens, he reckoned, was an appropriate time to get the facts of life. The trouble was, it focused more on the plumbing than the computer system that drives us. We feared it was not lounge room table literature and buried it deep beneath old jumpers in a drawer. It never had quite the appeal of *Man Junior*.

Generally, despite the fact that, in the 1930s, Mallee women fielded teams of Aussie rules football, I heard nothing of it and gender separation was the rule in sport. But there was a minor deviation because on Saturdays, I was drawn into a bit of gender bending. A shortage of female players in the B-grade competition meant that a boy under twelve could play as a woman. This presented a dilemma. Well used to spending lonely hours belting a tennis ball against the railway goods shed and indulging in frequent upper body exercise, I had developed a punishing serve. Was I obliged to observe restraint in my gender transformation? The problem was that opponents soon noticed I had no backhand, and no manner of agility from Lenny, my much older partner, could compensate.

The Last of the Knucklemen

Apart from the lack of any potentially maturing relationship with girls, and in the absence of male peers in town, I relied on adults no matter how short-lived that relationship might be. Some even unwittingly acted as models – if approval of their status or behaviour can qualify them as such. Billy Bent was one. Word was that he was a Mallee boxing champion at a time when north-west Victoria was several times more closely settled than it is today. In the local butcher shop, he stood a tall six foot or more with muscular forearms and broad shoulders and, on occasions when I saw him walking, he had the bounce in his step that was to me irrefutable evidence of his boxing prowess. Nothing of this meshed with my belief that boxers had to be aggressive, for he was decidedly not so. On the contrary, his behaviour towards Carl Altman the reclusive German in the bush, and Dave Rowan on the town fringes indicated kindness if not empathy.

Perhaps the fracas around the beer barrel at the silo was not the exception I thought it to be because a less than novel observation is that our values and even political attitudes and behaviour are driven by culture as well as genes. There is always a context. Boxing was no exception. Being able to defend oneself was an ethos widespread in 1940s rural Australia but it went back much further. Originating in ancient Greece, the activity reappeared in bare-knuckle contests in eighteenth-century England. It was not unexpected that in nineteenth-century Australia, a British colony, originally peopled by the rougher sort, men settling disputes with fists was the norm. Bare-knuckle fights still occur in the UK today but in official bouts, by the early twentieth century, a desire to protect both hands and head meant gloves were used.

I witnessed an exception to this. In a throwback to the bare-knuckled era, there was an unseemly beer-fuelled brawling contest outside a dance in our Memorial Hall. Two local men laid claims to a young woman. She sat patiently with others along a seat at the edge of the dance floor, oblivious of how far her suitors were willing to go to win her affection. With rising anger and taunts, the prospective combatants decided to settle their claims and move outside. The light was dim, part moonlight, part fugitive rays from the hall. No canvas ring, just uneven and sloping ground. Billy Bent's reputation as boxer and gentleman made him an obvious choice as referee. Stripped to the waist, sweat glistening on their white flesh in the moonlight, the two flailed about wildly in gloveless drunken contest, circling around looking for an opening then grunting and hissing, puffing forward to land a blow. Unsurprisingly, in a small community, I knew one of them and looked on in ghoulish yet fearful fascination. A fist smacking into nose brought blood that spread across one of the fighter's cheek. The bout inconclusive, Billy stepped in and told them to shake hands and sober up. It occurred to me that had they done so at the outset, they might have considered other ways to stake their claim but, as local argot would have it, 'The beer was talkin'.'

Some of my induction into the manly art of self-defence occurred in fun because, in sparring with Dad, any blows aimed at him he easily deflected with skilful turning of elbows and forearms. He confirmed the truth that prior experience in boxing could still sit very comfortably alongside a steady and generous temperament. With this sort of initiation, we lay on the floor and glued ourselves to the Kriesler to listen intently to world heavyweight bouts. We were willing to put up with the American caller's voice coming in waves with the ebb and flow of signal strength and spitting static. A lull, a brief quiet as the boxers waited for an opening, then a rise to a frenzy as one fighter got on top. Until 1949, the Brown Bomber, heavyweight boxer Joe Louis, reigned, only to cede the position to Jersey Joe Walcott. Again the latter was also an African-American, as many boxing champions of all weights have been.

As for the Aboriginal community, boxing has been the avenue to wealth and fame for poor minorities. Among the panoply of greats, the names Jack Johnson, Gene Tunney, Max Schmelling and Primo Carnera swam around in our consciousness. Clearly, Europeans could box too.

Radio serials such as *Dick Barton, Special Agent* had a similar capacity to draw us into the world outside. The planning, intrigue and heroic efforts of Barton and his accomplices Jock and Snowy enthralled me for most of my primary school years and the debut of secondary, broadly the period when he the Brown Bomber was king.

For decades, boxing troupes toured rural Australia, among them Jimmy Sharman's. He used to set up tent at the Ouyen Showground Fair alongside the coconut shy, the lucky numbers booth and the shooting gallery. To the background skirl of bagpipes out on the oval, one of Sharman's three boxers, often Aboriginal, pounded a bass drum to a much deeper beat. George Bracken, former Australian lightweight champion, started his career that way. Sharman's men stood up above eye level on a raised platform, resplendent in their silk dressing gowns, confident and menacing, arms folded, feet astride in high laced-up boots. Silently, they beckoned – taunted even – young locals to 'have a go!' for a few quid. Jimmy's men were hardened professionals and their daring challengers were often fuelled with Dutch courage. I wanted to join the crowd surging inside the tent but was held back by the feeling that it was not for young kids.

Boxing was meant to be a skill, a combination of physical fitness and calculated manoeuvre, not an impulsive reaction to perceived slights. If boxers have a curriculum vitae, my own bouts could only be deemed a one-all draw. The first began when I took offence at Butchy's taking my cap and teasing me in front of Mrs Dickie's shop. Cap-wearing was something my absorption in English *Billy Bunter* and *Film Fun* comics said was the thing to do. Right through school, I was fair game for those who got their kicks from teasing someone with a volatile temperament and thin skin. Nor was it helpful being youngest in the class. Very quickly, I felt it was only by using my fists against the older, bigger opponent that I could express my annoyance. Butchy was not the aggressive type and, if I had thought about it, his teasing was not how he usually behaved. He retaliated but his ineffective defence and backward stepping around the corner told me I won. Regrettably, although I was engaged in no other fight in Walpeup, my conduct at secondary school left something to be desired.

At the then Ouyen Higher Elementary School, if two boys began fighting, they had to settle the quarrel with boxing gloves during lunchtime. Teachers just turned a blind eye. As if in anticipation of a brawl, the sports cupboard even kept four sets. Tommy Williams was older than I was and he was bigger, heavier and, well, in my view, decidedly unlikeable. Discretion should have told me to walk away and ignore the goading of a number of bus travellers who gulped down their lunch to watch the anticipated event. The fact that they had little time for Tommy was irrelevant. In the heat of the noon sun, we thrashed around for a while but too many of his blows brought the smell of gloves too close to my nose and I had to admit he won.

There was another bout – not directly involving me – but one involving my friend Ian, the son of a road grader driver, with whom I stayed overnight after the school social. Suspended under his veranda he had a punching ball. He could pound it with either fist, bouncing it off the backboard with blurring professional speed. The other combatant was Brendan from my class (Ian from the one above). Not a close friend but popular and friendly nevertheless, Brendan was the one with a knack of disarming diminutive Miss Walton our music teacher. Ian pounded him relentlessly. He became just another punchball, well defeated, not something that went down well with many onlookers. Ian was quiet, introverted even, a trait that left him behind in the popularity stakes. Although I was unaware of it at the time, this was probably resonating with an element of my make-up.

Every Town Needs a Focus

Silo, railway station, tennis courts, football oval all had some social function. Nothing did so more than the hall completed on 16 May 1923 to honour the memory of soldiers killed in World War I. Similar structures to this red-brick building stood in other country towns. With its identifying Memorial Hall, enclosed in an architrave, ours paid faint homage to the Greek Acropolis although without the Elgin Marbles. Many farmers' sons made a heavy human investment in both world wars and honour rolls inside halls like ours bore the names of those killed. Often they were brothers. Although he was not a resident of our town at the time of his war service, a photo of Dad and fellow, but local, World War I soldiers appeared on the wall of the supper room, which was a less dignified construction tacked on the end of the hall. The diggers' photo I saw as both recognition of their war service and their contribution to the town. Older brother Ian enlisted from Boinka, further west along the highway.

Anzac Day reminded us that our hall was a Memorial Hall. It was widely believed in 1918 that no more would the world be embroiled in such conflict, yet in 1939, the year of a disastrous bushfire, and also my birth, that is what happened. Dad curiously spoke of Fritzy as if he were an occasionally hostile neighbour. There was no mention of the fact that his grandfather was born in Germany. No mention either of the bans imposed on the learning of German in schools, or people of German descent interned as enemy aliens, in all, a hostile environment that led some to change their names.

Out of the terrifying conflict, humour survived, and for Dad, it seemed no mask for deeper neurosis or grief. I heard nothing of the ear-shattering explosions, or even the smell of gas that was the reason for his small pension. They were not the sort of things old soldiers talked about. Two sculpted eighty-millimetre shells holding dust-covered bulrushes sat on our mantelpiece. A less obvious souvenir was his German belt. But then one day, I saw a wartime pistol in the garage. It disappeared as soon as I found it.

During our own children's war, we fired marbles to knock over cards bearing photos of the hated Nazi figures: Goering, Goebbels, Himmler, Bormann and, of course, Hitler. These cards did not match the ideological sophistication of the British in whose children's books, I was told, evil-looking badgers represented the German enemy. Come 1945, the European and Pacific wars over, we still dug trenches in the backyard covered with galvanised iron, bits of linoleum and dirt. Cylindrical batteries ten centimetres long doubled as hand grenades or walkie talkies (two-way radios).

As in Britain, where rationing gave rise to a paradoxical rise in community health, our post-war diet also had few luxuries. If the longevity of one's siblings was ultimately testament to a healthy childhood diet, we were not hard done by. Food always seems to loom large in my consciousness. Mum helped. No doubt she believed in keeping us healthy and when she found overt displays of affection difficult if not impossible, provision of food was a way of showing she cared.

Around war's end, some food items had yet to appear, bananas not until later. But we never went hungry. Two special delights stand out. For a summer evening treat, Dad took great pleasure in suggesting we run down to Mrs Dickie's to order little rectangular bricks of Sennitt's ice cream that we held between thin wafers. They were no bigger than samplers designed to whet the appetite. But there were other treats. Neatly packed compressed dried fruit and nuts that Ian brought home from service in New Guinea gave new meaning to iron rations. In taste and source, to me they were exotic.

For a previous three months on Timor, vastly outnumbered by Japanese, Ian's company never knew where wartime deprivation would pitch the allegiance of local Timorese. Food for Ian was scarce. It surprised me to hear that he ran close to being court martialled for 'speeding up' the distribution of the meagre supplies. His willingness to endure such privations was surely about the prevailing patriotism but also his hatred of boring, soulless labour on a farm that never promised a pleasant or economically rewarding life.

He returned from Timor and New Guinea with a complete package of tropical diseases along with his professed residual hatred for the Japanese soldiers. He knew about, if he did not witness, the loss of his fellow troops at their hands in often atrocious circumstances. As in Vietnam, it was also sometimes difficult to identify the enemy. He recounted the time when, on patrol in Timor with a fellow Australian, he stumbled on a rock at the very moment when the spear thrown by a local Timorese cut through the air space previously occupied by his head. It did cause him to reflect on the role of luck in life: accident, genetic heritage, economic conditions, fortunate encounters – all the elements shaping personality and opportunity. Although some Timorese were persuaded to throw in their lot with the Japanese, many Australian soldiers owed their survival to the locals, either in their provision of sustenance or acting as impromptu medical orderlies for the injured. The Timorese paid dearly for it. Forty thousand of them died at the hands of the Japanese.

I remember, just twenty-five years since the war to end all wars, families gathered on Anzac Day, 25 April, to mourn lost sons, husbands, brothers, sometimes up to three of them. Women in best hats and dark dresses and men with suntanned hands, necks and faces chafing in collar and tie, conversed in funereal undertones at the entrance of the Memorial Hall. A woman furtively dabbed away tears. Brief words were exchanged. On a gramophone, a soprano's rendition of 'Ave Maria' echoed down the hall, the signal to move inside. Silently, people paused at the end of the hard wooden benches as others slid along to make room.

With the hall nearly full, about thirty ex-servicemen and seven ex-servicewomen of both wars, all in civvies but with medals fastened to lapels, moved in to the place of honour in front rows.

I lost no father, brother, uncle, nor any in women's ranks, yet unformed as I was, I could not escape the pall of grief. Some sat hunched and tense, sniffling back tears. The whole ceremony – a soldier reading the names of the fallen; the Lord's Prayer and 'Abide with Me' – resonated with authority and sadness. During Bach's Air on a G String, my eyes watered, all control gone. I felt embarrassed and unprepared for the Last Post and Reveille. Just outside the side door, Mr Nulty puffed and squeaked his tortuous progress over the notes on his trumpet. Giggles rippled through the rows of kids to the hall's side. Many seemed to be discomforted by the solemnity of proceedings and the grief of adults in front of them. The mangling of the time-honoured trumpet expression of mourning, awakening and hope triggered a release. That aside, whenever I hear the other two pieces of music, I am again gripped by emotion.

Community singing in the hall or, to my youngest ears, empty singing, was anything but empty. Retiring as she was, Mrs McCurdy played a pivotal role. Our local pianist, she sat shrouded in the dim light of a lamp suspended on the top of an old piano to the right of the stage. No vibrato, no crescendo, she pounded the keys while adults and children alike belted out the words of such hardy World War I favourites as 'Lili Marlene', 'Pack up your Troubles', 'Tipperary' and 'Coming in on a Wing and a Prayer'. The words of such songs locals had carefully inscribed on glass slides, each in their own distinctive lettering.

Although small communities depend on the reliability of their volunteers, their efforts are not totally altruistic. No matter what satisfaction there is in contributing, the alternative is to sit bored mindless and friendless at home. A reliably civic-minded local was Rex Warren, who operated the electric slide lantern projecting the transcribed words onto a large sheet which doubled as a screen. Like a budding Barbirolli, Ellis, one of the Golding brothers, stood on the stage beside the curtain, beating his torch in rough time to the music. Occasionally he shone it on the words for those who only too obviously were being left behind. Although not alone in my lack of musical talent, singing with others brought an elemental pleasure – as it continues to do with choristers today. Some would blanch at the comparison but playing for a higher goal – literally and figuratively – in a footy team also somehow focused me outside myself and had similar emotional appeal.

Community singing had other elements besides singing and it never disappointed me. One of them was a quiz for which Dad prepared questions. Risking the charge of insider trading, I sought in typical fashion to show how clever I was by trying to answer the easier questions, some of which were reserved for kids. No one was to be left out. The reward for those with the correct answer was a packet of steamrollers flung across the audience. Participants therefore had to be able to catch as well as answer questions. Bear in mind that this was remote Mallee in the decade 1945–55, when most of the older folk lacked extended formal education. Nevertheless, like Mrs Varney, a regular in the audience, heavy figure, her greying hair pinned in a circle and bun at the back, some read extensively, especially history and biography. It was not surprising that Ellis, doubling up as quizmaster as well as singing compère, habitually looked in her direction for the answer to a more difficult question.

Most Saturday-night community singings featured an item, often a short play put on by the Younger Set, most in their twenties, along with an occasional older one who had enduring thespian aspirations. No theatre groups came to town and pictures (movies) were only screened once a month, so it was a matter of make your own fun or go without. As kids, we sat in the two front rows, listening to last-minute whispered instructions on stage while waiting for curtain rise. Remarkably, we were prepared to sit patiently staring up at a washed-out romantic scene on the curtain, a lone boat on a lake surrounded by misty trees, with a mountain backdrop. All were enclosed in a circle as if we were looking through a telescope. Patience rewarded, little jabs appeared in the curtain, sounds of things being dragged across the stage, and audible, earnest whispers.

'No, that's too close. Put it over there.'

'Jenny, you've got buttons undone.'

'Don't forget Clarrie, when Jenny says, "I'm not going to put up with this any more," that's when you come in. And don't forget, you only try to kiss her on the cheek.'

'Ladies and gentlemen,' Ellis announced, 'the Walpeup Younger Set is about to present a sketch called "Keep your drawers clean, Henry".'

This prompted guffaws from two teenagers in the second row.

As with the items, much of the entertainment was locally generated. It helped us to accept if not understand one another and reinforced relationships. Above all, it generated a tolerance of performances never likely to threaten those on Broadway. Much anticipated was Andrew's reading of the local newspaper, in reality creative doggerel pinned to the inside of the *Ouyen and District North-west Express*. Any minor accident, mistake or failure involving a known citizen was inflated and distorted to create maximum amusement. It was the literary equivalent of a melodrama in which locals were the actors, and I was to play a part. To my chagrin, I scored a black eye while fielding for the local men's cricket team at Thursday evening's practice. As I chased ball to the boundary, it hit a tuft of grass and smacked me in the eye. By Saturday, my eye was a halo of blues, greens and black. Naturally, that made the news, but for me, the pain gone, the item achieved the desired effect. I was briefly the centre of attraction.

Since Walpeup was well off the Melbourne Symphony Orchestra's circuit, we had to draw on local musical talent. There was no auditioning, no elaborate CV demanded, just gratitude for someone who would enliven our existence. A few instruments dominated. Many had an accordion of either piano or button type. Marmaduke the swagman, camped beside the football ground, earned a guest spot for his abilities with the harmonica. There was something incongruous in this scruffy figure whom most in a tiny town did not know and those who did ignored, holding an audience with skills few possessed. Did this facility say something about his past? I wonder. Typically, I never asked.

No one came on stage with a harp or double bass, but at least use was made of local materials. Among the return acts was music made by drawing a bow across a saw held between the knees. In the grip of a dedicated practitioner, it had a sort of torturous potential. For another act, a farmer coaxed a tune from a folded gum leaf that was painfully not suited to bass notes. His challenge was to select a young leaf flexible and thin enough to vibrate but not to break mid-performance.

No age was too young to start life before the footlights. Four years old, I joined other local kids in a rendition of *Snow White and the Seven Dwarfs*. For several weeks after school, Mrs McCurdy, dear maternal figure with grey hair, rubbery lips and wayward dentures, had us rehearsing our singing while she played the hall piano. Unfortunately, come our debut, the well-meaning addition of more lamps on this very hot summer's night produced rotisserie-like temperatures. Not long into our act, perspiration began to dribble down our faces, its path marked by ever denser colouring from our crêpe paper headgear. As we marched off to the final 'Hi ho', the loud reception signified appreciation of extraordinary talent or, more likely, bug-eyed parents' cloying support for their little cherubs.

Socialisation in such a small community was not confined to biological parents. More than once, Mrs McCurdy offered motherly instruction to us young kids. She was the one who lived next door in a still operational bakery put to use by her husband, the ex-army cook.

The last song on the community singing program signalled lights on. Men and boys launched into stacking heavy wooden forms at the end of the hall ready for dancing. Long as well as heavy, they demanded someone on each end and thus a chance for boys to work with men. First, there was a ritual preparation of the deep red hardwood floor with a generous sprinkling of sawdust, kerosene and ground-up candle.

This was the signal for us boys to drag one another up and down the hall on a wheat bag to ensure that the magic combination of substances was ground in. Better fun still was to run full tilt towards the other end, put on the brakes, slide and turn in one motion, and with legs striving to gain traction, begin propelling ourselves back again. This behaviour, tolerated by adults, had the veneer of being necessary floor conditioning but was basically a time for boys to show off. Again, adults and girls indulgently looked on while boys amused themselves.

Dances in the hall, whether run by the footy club or simply to round off community singing, played out a time-honoured ritual. Women and girls lined one side of the hall, chatting to one another and feigning indifference to dancing. Blokes sought comfort in numbers at the entrance while stealing surreptitious glances towards the assembled beauties. Finally, with deep breath, courage summoned, and their eye on a partner, they would stride across no-man's-land with studied casualness.

At the foot of the stage, two pairs of farmer brothers provided the music: drums, piano and saxophone, the latter, in the 1940s and 1950s, a favourite instrument at dances. For an accomplished musician, a rendition on the sax of 'Golden Wedding' later became a cameo performance. Not quite rising to these heights, Brian Wagner's playing produced a tantalising blend of fugitive squeaks and the mellow tones it was designed for. One brother from each pair shared duties on the piano. Taking his turn as pianist, Andrew Golding seemed to feel that bouncing on his seat like someone testing mattress springs would enhance rhythm. Certainly it was unmistakeable evidence of his zeal. Ray, Brian's brother, who job-shared on the piano with Andrew, smoked as he played. Over time, the evidence of his right-handedness lay in black holes in the high note keys caused by his smouldering cigarette butts. Ellis Golding's drumming was more symbolic than real. He favoured caressing the pigskin with fine wire brushes over drumsticks, not unlike his performance on the football field – more promise than execution. Earlier on a Saturday, curly hair streaming behind him, he would tear after the ball like a cheetah and run straight past it, mumbling of the game he dare not bite, as the satirical poet put it. As the evening progressed, the musicians' periodic retreats outdoor for beer enhanced the tempo markedly, not that this was of concern to dancers.

Down in the supper room, the lean-to at the end of the hall behind the stage, one could hear, 'Six clubs' then 'Six hearts' and 'Seven no trumps' in quick succession. Two rows of old folk sat rugged up, playing convivial games of five hundred or euchre. Game over, a brief 'If I'd played my ace of diamonds first...' a laugh and they changed position and opponent.

Rex Warren, earlier on the slide lantern and probably in his forties, neither played cards nor danced. Courteous, more than passably handsome and previously a polished footballer in a culture in which that counted, he seemed happy to just patiently tend the open fire. Periodically, he shone his torch through the steam onto saveloys rising and falling like red dugongs in the square four-gallon bucket. Shy perhaps, he always talked to me, one of several adults I depended on for conversation.

For the old folks, the open fire was the only heating but I heard no complaint. Goldings, Warrens, Wagners, the ethos of volunteering often ran in families.

Besides community singing, the hall for a short period housed several energetic table tennis players and briefly a young farm worker seeking unsuccessfully to promote boxing lessons. His target audience was clearly too small and his interest soon waned. With television still years away, the screening of movies or pictures projected by Nulty's cinema from Ouyen required much less active participation and had more universal appeal. This monthly dose of culture was a BIG EVENT for which people willingly endured long wooden bum-numbing seats, the ones used for Anzac services and community singing. Happy children commanded front rows for an uninterrupted view. Glowing rods of carbon on the projector produced the necessary light but sometimes it flickered ominously and as chirpy soprano screen voices descended into deepest contralto the audience was plunged into silence and darkness. While a month's wait for movie night generated a store of patience, a young male voice would still feel compelled to call out, 'Put a penny in it.'

We had no movie serials and television only came to city screens a year after I left Walpeup. Our heroic figures Hopalong Cassidy, Tom Mix and the Phantom only appeared in the printed version.

If I had to choose, I would not have selected the *Phantom of the Opera* as the first movie to watch. A hooded man swinging from a chandelier to ominous heavy chords from Liszt's first piano concerto immediately struck fear into me. It set me sneaking a look through gaps between fingers. It got worse. I tried viewing from the corner of my eye, then under my elbow. Soon it was all too much. I tiptoed down to the men standing near the door, where they could duck out for a smoke. Wedged between two of the biggest adults and now a distance from the screen, I felt emboldened to watch until with relief it ended. Bruce and I raced home. Friendly familiar daytime trees and buildings now harboured a multitude of evil figures.

Breathless, we went inside to tell Mum, by now in bed, that we were back.

She gathered that I'd not had the most comforting experience. In a memorably affectionate gesture, she asked, 'Would you like to come into our bed?'

An early onset of male ego and pride prompted me to declare that we would be quite comfortable in the sleepout. Just over three years my senior, Bruce had already decided he would head there as usual. This place of rest with its cement-sheet walls, fly wire in the top half, galvanised-iron roof and fly-wire door, gave adequate space for our two beds.

We were not long in bed when an unaccountable snorting and rumbling confirmed our worst fears that the town's benign daytime appearance was anything but that by night. The noise grew louder.

Soon, several black shapes with an inhumanly number of legs, very visible through the screen door, clomped on the concrete apron between us and the house. A few minutes passed and we waited breathlessly. The sound died away and, heart pounding, I raced inside to take up our mother's offer.

It is important to state that livestock, sometimes fattening up before slaughter, wandered freely around town untroubled by fences which were often falling into disrepair. The town's land was in effect a sort of commons in which livestock for sale and domestic cows like our Molly found forage.

In the absence of many young ones my age, I spent much time with Bruce. He provided greater strength if ever that was needed and was an antidote to my impulsivity. He had a couple of childhood friends but together we trapped rabbits, played tennis all summer holidays, bottled fruit, kicked the footy and listened to test cricket, world heavyweight boxing and radio serials.

This is not to say we were alike. He generous to a fault, I having scoffed my half of our Old Jamaica chocolate would look longingly at his until he gave me some. He was uncomplicated and transparent, I devious. He difficult to arouse, I hot-tempered. I had no grounds for being critical of him, although I do confess being a little jealous that my temperament and behaviour incurred more of our mother's wrath than anything he did or said.

Mum must have realised she had two very different kids on her hands and one day her perception was confirmed in full light. Bruce and I were throwing chips of Mallee root over the shed where old Mr Kendrew mended boots safely away from the demands of his wife. We were taking turns. Unfortunately, just as I unleashed my missile, Bruce stepped in front. It struck him on the side of his head and blood began to flow. I was mortified. The blow brought his understandable howls of distress and Mum tore out of the house in full fury. Accusing me of being hot-tempered – a bit rich in the circumstances – she sent me to bed without any dinner. For me, deprivation of a meal was punishment in the extreme. Explanations were useless. No amount of indignant protestation helped. Having on other occasions given vent to temper displays, my reputation brought me down.

Where my brother and I also differed was in the rewards schooling brought us. The attitudes and teaching methods employed did not match his personality, needs or abilities – nor those of nearly everyone else. As a result, he left school relatively early, following the precedent of other boys in the district. Life out of school for all of them had more appeal than life in it. When I was thirteen, he left for Melbourne, where it was possible for him to quit one job on Friday and pick up another on Monday. The youngest of five, I was now an only child.

Grief and Diversions

In small communities, just as the role of socialising the young was to a degree shared, so too was grief. We had a connection with the death of a young girl, probably no more than four. She was the daughter of one of the families whose mail and bread we delivered. Sadly, when she craned her head out a half-open car window to look at a pig, she slipped and strangled herself. Not yet ten myself, I was overwhelmed by the combination of raw grief and the dignity of the grieving mother as we gathered near the cavernous hole in the local cemetery. It seemed to match the gaping hole in the parents' hearts. A day of black clothes, black thoughts, and one of unrealised potential.

By contrast, the death of my ninety-three-year-old grandmother had no comparable emotional impact. I was now older and maybe I sensed it was something of a relief for Mum. I already shared the view that the death of someone at the beginning of life was of greater consequence than one at the end.

Growing up in the '40s and '50s was not all obedient solemnity. It involved risk-taking, as well as earning and learning. In addition to relying on Marmaduke being no Olympic sprinter and Mrs Dickie's being unable to stem the loss of her diminishing stock of indigestible licorice and gobstoppers, there was always playing with fireworks, or crackers as we called them, especially double-bungers.

One night, heading down a moonlit road after community singing with two older blokes, Bruce and I mounted a double-bunger on the front post of David Brown's place. He was the kid both younger and better footballer than I and I suspect that our choice of this gatepost wasn't totally accidental. We lit it and the first explosion sent it spiralling toward the window of his baby brother sleeping in the front bedroom, where it detonated again. He burst into loud howls; lights flashed on; father Robert pounded along the corridor as we raced full tilt down the road, followed by the angry father's abuse. We had a good start but decided to head through uncleared scrub bordering the Methodist church and, to be doubly sure, split up. Without evidence of any misdemeanour, Bruce and I slid quietly into bed in the sleepout. Mr Brown no doubt had his suspicions because the pool of potential villains was small.

Crackers and rockets were such fun. Every 5 November, on a vacant block beside McIntosh's place in a town where land wasn't at a premium, we would build a bonfire in honour of Guy Fox (Guy Fawkes). In 1605 he failed in his attempt to blow up the English Houses of Parliament, a rather undemocratic way of settling differences. From all corners of the town, we dragged into a pile, branches, old paling fences and bits of linoleum, anything vaguely flammable. Once or twice, someone made a crude effigy of the disgruntled seventeenth-century Catholic.

Mostly, the night-time blaze was no more than an excuse to let off penny bungers, spinning wheels, rockets and Tom Thumbs. These smallest of crackers came in two rows linked with their fuses like rows of pigs at a trough. Unfortunately, someone threw a cracker at Bobby Wilson. It hit his pocket where he had his Tom Thumbs. Then followed the unedifying spectacle of his dancing around frantically slapping his thigh trying to stop the crackers going off like the machine guns we heard on radio serials. Some saw him as a bully and laughed.

We tried them all: sending tins into the air with penny bungers, listening to the 'whoosh' as a cracker exploded inside a bottle, and aiming rockets at a nearby street lamp. None, however, created quite the reverberation of a bottle of petrol thrown on a fire down in the scrub. We never needed Guy Fawkes for an excuse to light a fire.

David was no paragon of virtue and surely not what his mother believed him to be. One thing he and most of us at secondary school were very good at was throwing: cricket balls, tennis balls, softballs, and always stones. Perhaps it came from a desire to make a mark on the world. Regrettably, it was literally the case for David and me.

There was a bountiful supply of such stones along the railway line – beautiful, smooth, water-worn quartz specimens put there as stabilising ballast and to tempt us. Conveniently, flat as the Mallee terrain was, there was still need to elevate the railway line to maintain an even gradient. This meant that the cache of stones was nearly at the same level as the insulators on the telephone poles running parallel with the railway line. It was a cinch! When practice improves performance, the constant throwing ensured we were accurate.

By this stage, our frontal lobes were not fully developed and inhibition was lacking. As a result, the criminal nature of shattering insulators didn't cross our minds. It did that of the constabulary from Ouyen because Mr Plod had a serious discussion with Dad – as befitting one of the respectable and respected parents. I had no difficulty guessing why the policeman was favouring us with a visit. I could have paid dearly for my irresponsibility. He could have pulled out his dog-eared *Criminal Offences, Revised Edition 1947*. Wilful damage? Committing a public nuisance? Destruction of government property? Any number of charges would have been justified. Unfortunately, too often my behaviour was characterised by recklessness followed by fairly serious remorse.

Live targets had a particular appeal. It is harder to hit one that is moving than a stationary one like an insulator, especially a young chook sensing it is in mortal danger. The owner of several of these, very elderly Mrs Surrerier, mother of either Mr or Mrs McCurdy next door, would have been a shoo-in for the part of one of the witches in Macbeth. At the sound of chickens in distress, she was wont to show her staring eyes and tangled white hair above the boundary paling fence like a puppet from a Punch and Judy show. For good reason, she was concerned about the welfare of her racing model White Leghorns. Their desire for a delectably enriched diet in our garden, and ours for a continuous supply of vegetables, were bound to come into conflict. Protective of my gardening efforts, I developed the art of estimating the fleeing birds' speed as I threw any stones I could get my hands on.

If I scored a hit, the chook would leap squawking into the air with gravity-defying ease then continue running and flapping seemingly unharmed. When I started using a shanghai, it was like changing from bow and arrow to AK47. Still, there were no fatalities and the missiles seem to have no salutary effect on the marauding interlopers either because our garden was too big a prize or poultry communication wasn't very effective.

Not all invading species were defenceless. The town always had a big problem with cats, especially howling toms that had the habit of stinking the place out before they had the temerity to die underneath the house, from where extraction was difficult. Even the local butcher, Billy Bent, armed himself with bow and arrow to wage war on them. His choice of weapon was not voluntary because discharging a firearm in a built-up area was illegal. Rather than engaging in the sensible act of either desexing or dispatching such toms and tabbies with the green dream (a lethal injection), people allegedly just dropped them off from the train as they journeyed westward from Ouyen to Pinnaroo. Whatever their origins, cats breed like rabbits – or almost. One female can produce up to fifteen kittens a year. Heaven knows how many of the birds, small reptiles and mammals cats killed. Especially was this so when they became truly feral and assumed the proportions of a small lynx and swelled rumours that panthers were roaming the woods.

With a developing love of birds – despite my stealing eggs for my collection – I was definitely ambivalent about the cat species and remain so. Yet I always had my own, including black and white Whiskey, who would willingly double as a scarf when I sat in the winter sunshine. On one occasion when Whiskey was just an endearing little fluff-ball, a wild kitten emerged from beneath the house to lap up – and steal – milk I'd laid out for my pet. Frustrated by the smells, the night howling, the wanton breeding of these invading animals, I launched myself horizontally from the elevation of washhouse steps in best rugby tackle, arms outstretched to pounce on the invader. It recoiled, deeply offended, and sank its teeth into the back of my hand. Before it fled,

The author, Whiskey and Bruce, 1948.

the animal inflicted retribution. Bacteria which the beast injected into my hand ensured that I suffered for many weeks thereafter. Cats are not fond of brushing their teeth and nor do they ever visit a manicurist.

As a country boy, I lived with the killing of animals. It seemed to us that the only means of tackling the cat problem was to put tiny unwanted kittens in a sugar bag, plunge it into a bucket of water and hold it and contents down with a brick until the bubbling stopped. It involved an immediate blocking of empathy and quite contradictory behaviour given my fondness for Whiskey. Still, we had no other way of addressing the problem. A cat wounded with gunshot or arrow stood to suffer much more. I also accepted the slaughter of animals – the sheep, cattle and pigs – the basis of the almost constant servings of meat we enjoyed. When a rabbit was squealing piteously in agony in one of my steel-jawed traps, I had no compunction about quickly bending its head back and snapping its neck. That was quick. The potentially night-long agony was certainly not so but rabbit traps were widely accepted and, as shown by the example of Dave Rowan, were the source of a livelihood for thousands across the continent.

Cars provided their share of risk and fun. One Saturday night, after a meal of regulation steak and eggs and a few songs on their jukebox at the only Ouyen cafe, a number of us piled into Nobbie's Austin A40 sedan. The local sports ground had a circular bike track. What was wrong with doing a circuit? The folly of this idea soon became apparent as we generated speed, because a large roller loomed in our tracks. Too late to brake, the only option was to wrench the car back into the centre, momentarily on two wheels before we slowed down on the oval surface and resumed breathing.

Butchy Sidney acquired a T-Model Ford. The absence of hood, and air rushing through our hair as we did early versions of burnouts in slow motion, just reinforced the fun. Did he or Nobbie have a driving licence? I doubt it and yet the only police officer had a beat in Nobbie's home town. Apocryphal or not but when an Ouyen resident allegedly approached the policeman to get a licence, he was asked to drive the friendly plod to the pub, where it was duly filled out. When I was still a fifteen or sixteen-year-old, driving my mother to Red Cliffs, I had momentary heart palpitations to see the law's representative pulling alongside. He looked across at me, absent-mindedly doing a little brain surgery. Apparently his mind was on a big case, possibly word of another sheep stealing, because he continued on his way.

No age seemed too young in the district for a boy to start driving on the road. But being in charge of a bulk truckload of wheat arguably added to the risk. One day, a farmer's son, barely a teenager and scarcely able to see over the wheel, rolled up alone at the weighbridge with sixty bags in bulk. Possibly he was advised to wait until he was older before continuing because that was the only time I saw him in that position.

Utes (utility vehicles) were as indispensable as vehicles for carrying small loads in the late 1940s and early 1950s When we rode to the Coleman twins' farm in their father's ute, nothing stopped us from being tossed out. Seat belts did not become compulsory until fifteen years after I left Walpeup, and prohibitions on riding in the back of utes even later. These vehicles were ideal vehicles for fox shooting. While one stood up directing a spotlight onto the invasive pest, his companion did the shooting. For my only experience, no restraining belts were worn, despite rough terrain that threatened to toss us out and discharge my companion's loaded rifle and shotgun.

Risks confront the farmer all the time. As a result of fatigue or simple inattention, one cocky out north of town severed half his right hand while cutting chaff. Just days after admission to hospital, a normal right-hander, he wrote a letter home with his left hand. Near his farm and elsewhere, winding roads were not always laid down with lines of sight in mind. Tragically, the neighbour and best friend of the man with no fingers on his right hand headed down his driveway and crashed into him coming around a bend. Death was instant but not the suffering of the survivor.

Secondary Schooling, a Process of Attrition

Still not yet eleven, I began catching a school bus to take me to Ouyen Higher Elementary School. Conveniently, it stopped at our front door. Starting at Underbool, fifteen kilometres to the west, it made stops at Torrita, Walpeup, Tiega, Galah and finally Ouyen, in total, a distance of forty-five kilometres.

I never saw a town for Tiega even though some kids identified as Tiega residents. But it had a footy team: white with a red V, composed mainly of farmers, it seemed. Each morning, three Poole brothers, school bags slung over shoulders, would come into view, trudging through the mirage across the treeless plain to the bus like early explorers crossing the desert.

The names of these tiny settlements always presented a challenge to newsreaders, particularly when they reported rainfall totals, for which Dad as postmaster had responsibility. (Occasionally, ours was inflated when I accidentally sprayed the gauge with the garden hose.) Walpeup became Walperp and the soft g of Tiega always defeated announcers who thought it had the hard sound of tiger. Some of the town names were doubtless Aboriginal in origin yet, like much in childhood, we just took them for granted.

The Poole brothers could attest that an enduring feature of their lives was small bush flies. These annoying insects were in their countless billions, nourished by cowpats in which they bred and found food. After I left Walpeup, the CSIRO introduced the dung beetle and it found the same cowpats particularly appetising. They quickly reduced pats to valuable fertiliser. Soon, deprived of food and lodging, fly numbers were reduced by ninety per cent. Until then, we put up with them. When one landed on Lacey's face, he'd deliver a killer blow and drag the carcase down his cheek between forefinger and thumb. By day's end, his face was covered with brown vertical streaks like remnant warpaint after a day's battle. Sometimes he dropped their bodies in his school inkwell or in the hole in Mrs Dickie's shop window where someone had hit it with a stone.

Motion sickness, partly brought on by the gravel road, and frequent headaches meant I often could not study for the fifty-minute bus journey to and from school. Reading *Blackhawk* comics and the occasional game of five hundred were popular. Motion sickness aside, it was still a much anticipated pleasure to cap off a week's toil with a turn at a copy of *Truth* newspaper. Often, truth-telling came second to salaciousness and sensationalism. In fact, it seemed an obligation. It featured stories of philandering, extortion, and the odd society murder told in lurid detail. Across its pages were draped photos of women who, if scantily clad, were tame by the standard of today's English tabloids. Even these distractions weren't enough to counter the noxious efflorescence emanating from Reggie's gut, so strong it sent us diving to the open windows. Given their predictability, it might have been wiser to suggest he lay off the hot chips. The potency of the emissions was remarkable. It even led the driver to pump the door to create a draft. Boys being boys, Reggie was not alone in this behaviour.

Ritual also played a part in our response to brown snakes that were native to the area and therefore perfectly entitled to cross a road intruding on their territory. For whatever reason, in two successive summers, a large specimen paused in the middle of the road and rose up in defiance. The response followed a pattern.

Whizzo, the driver (a corruption of his name, not a comment on his driving), would halt the bus and shout something like, 'Snake! A big bugger!'

Immediately, we'd rush to the windows. He would grab the bus broom, swing the door open and sail forth to combat. Each time, in bringing the broom down on the reptile's back, the rigid handle would snap. Even with a broken back, the snake's writhing indicated it still had fight. As if on cue, we would pile out of the bus and in primaeval frenzy, race to nearby Mallee trees. We would swing on a branch until it broke, and our noble warrior chief selected the stoutest one. He laid into the snake until all six feet of squirming ceased. Snake shoved to the side of the road, we stood around it in a circle, half in fear and wonderment at its sleek lines, its shiny overlocking scales and subtle underneath shades. For the rest of the journey and throughout the school day, each account of the event became more dramatic. It led to a surge of snake stories and a rare opportunity for the teller to hold the limelight.

Fear of snakes was always out of proportion to the injury and death they inflicted. Like most creatures, they became dangerous when they felt threatened. At that time, few humans gave a thought to their role in combating mice that could so quickly morph into plague proportions. Dad told of killing snakes with fencing wire or stock whip from his position mounted on a horse. We were probably enacting a time-honoured ritual, because every society or culture seems to have its Other, human or animal, something unambiguously evil. Demonising them creates heroes and brings people together.

Towards the end of my secondary school years, I was given a responsibility as a sort of long-service medal. I was made a bus prefect, in keeping with my status as a prefect at school. In the latter role, I recall doing absolutely nothing to promote social harmony or public good or demonstrate leadership qualities. If it was modelled on Hitler Youth, it failed dismally. On the bus, there was one practice that was beyond my capacity to influence. Apparent to even the least perceptive observer, girls matured both physically and emotionally more quickly in their early teens than boys. In the following troubling situation, the physical dimension was the more relevant because the emotional advance was questionable. Vivienne was a girl whose mind was perpetually on the opposite sex, usually adult men, and certainly not schoolwork. During the bus trip home, she found it flattering to sit on the engine cover beside the driver and face back down the bus interior.

While he leered into the rear-vision mirror as if to gain our approval, his left hand wandered to her knee, and inched its way upwards, much to her delighted giggles and feigned protestations. No matter that she was a willing participant, the collusion in this public display amounted to child abuse. Surely a measure of my own immaturity, I found it embarrassing but the thought of reporting it did not enter my head. Complicating it for me, in this incident, she was physically mature and I a sixteen-year-old male.

For the six years I rode the school bus, little topographical variety and interest marked our journey. In a word, the land was monotonously devoid of surprise. Out of respect for an unknown Frenchman, the only significant departure from the prevailing flatness and mixture of wheat fields and salty clay pans was Le Coutier's Hill. No gentle rise, descending it was like taking the Luna Park big dipper. As if such a hill was an offence to the dominant landscape, it had to go. Our daily bus trip was uneventful to say the least and nothing could have been better stage-managed for our entertainment than the decapitation of a hill. What occurred was not just boys' toys. Girls also stared out the bus window at the clanking, revving, army tank emitting bursts of smoke each time it butted a road grader – far bigger than those typically used on our roads. Towing the grader in the lead was a rubber-tyred tractor. It also dwarfed anything ploughing local paddocks. The mission of this giant trio was to level the only hill for miles around that ever excited conversation. I know I was not alone in wishing there were more hills to flatten.

The trouble was, removal erased both the hill and the chance of an addition to local folklore, as well, of course, as the thrill of sailing down its steep side. One Saturday night, scrub at its base became the unscheduled sleeping place for the Pensenbene twins. (At the time, I thought that only children could be twins.) Farmers of no apparent prosperity, these two brothers lived out east somewhere. With Dad and Dave-type soiled and baggy trousers secured with hay bands around the waist, bootlaces missing, check shirts, and dented hats carrying a generation of dust, their visits to town did excite a certain attention. Seventy per cent of men in this period smoked and they were no exception. What was distinctive about the Pensenbene twins was their use of cigarette holders – an image more like that used by 1920s flappers in magazines. Theirs was also a practice farmers would have secretly regarded as effeminate. The problem was that holders never left their mouths and created a furrow in the bottom lip and a convenient channel for a never-ending supply of spittle. Hence their nicknames: Dewdrop and April Showers.

The Pensenbenes were not alone in taking relief at the Victoria Hotel in Ouyen from the ardours of farming. Another Walpeup identity, Bill Torrego was also imbibing on the same night. Hotels at both Underbool and Ouyen enjoyed frequent patronage. The twins left the local alehouse at the end of liberal trading hours and, affected by their imbibing, careered off the road at the foot of Le Coutier's Hill. Rather than reverse out of trouble, they decided to sleep it off. Bill T, meanwhile, saw their old Buick tourer angled facing a big tree and an opportunity. He attached their front bumper bar to it with several strands of strong number 8 fencing wire. When the story got out, there was speculation about how long after waking they revved the vehicle in reverse before realising that they were not going anywhere

While Walpeup primary school was small, it had a high ceiling. I remember well the painter on plank and ladders way above our heads whistling the nineteenth-century tune 'He'd fly through the air with the greatest of ease, that daring young man on the flying trapeze'. Any distraction was welcome. By comparison with our primary school, Ouyen Higher Elementary School was palatial. Built in 1929 of Mount Gambier freestone, it was one of only two built of such material rather than weatherboard and glass as were many public schools subsequently. This limestone was formed from the sacrifice of millions of tiny marine fossils. They were still recognisable enough to interest more introverted non-footballing pupils not picked for a team. The main building comprised a rectangle of concrete blocks, open at one end. They still fitted closely enough not to trip us as we did civilising folk dancing in our senior years.

Up a rise stood woodwork and metalwork centres of the same stone with store rooms in between. Attached to the woodwork centre and at right angles lay a fortress-like toilet block. Towards my Matriculation year, the Education Department dumped two glass and wooden 'portables' between the craft blocks and main classrooms. Without air conditioning, and temperatures over the century for days, it gave me an early understanding of the term greenhouse effect, well before scientists began warning of its impact on global temperatures. So for buildings that was it. As mentioned, no library at school or anywhere in the district.

Initiation ceremonies or hazing can take pernicious forms. Our school fostered none of the brutality of English public schools or the Australian armed forces. For our initiation, newcomers had to endure having their head put under a running tap by senior boys. With the land shimmering under summer heat, it was like Brer Rabbit when he implored Brer Fox, 'PLEASE don't throw me into that briar patch!' – precisely where Rabbit would be safe from the predator. The gathering point for the would-be initiates was under the shade of two umbrella cedars. Conveniently, they supplied large quantities of seeds the size of small marbles giving much greater range than peppercorns for pea-shooters.

My first year class, Form 1 – the only lot of newcomers – contained forty-four students. By my final year in Form 6, there were two of us, a doctor's son and me. Another, the son of a Greek café proprietor, joined us during the year. If current football crowds witnessed the same attrition, imagine the furore. The reasons for this spectacular failure of the school to hold pupils were many. Significantly, only boys remained. Girls, including Shirley who was an able student, left for jobs in primary teaching and nursing, then seen as an extension of a traditional nurturing domestic role. I also mentioned earlier that some girls could see no further than marriage. Boys found ready employment in farming, labouring or local shops. The consoling thought was that Victor, a competent student of maths, might have found his skills useful to tally up the takings in his father's pie shop.

These then were the attracting forces or, in migration parlance, 'pull' factors. School itself quite successfully engineered some push factors. For the latter, its seeming irrelevance, especially to life on the land, was high on the list. What were aspiring farmers to make of the history of ancient Egypt, English grammar, or French? Probably, the way many subjects were taught was also not enough to excite enduring interest in them for their own sake. Was it reasonable to focus so heavily on assessment processes in which many learnt only too clearly that in what passed as worth – success in exams – they were less worthy than others? The method of handing out the foolscap exam papers amounted to organised public humiliation. It favoured the competitive and, shamefully, that often helped me. The saving grace was that some put little store by exam success anyway. Clearly, there could have been greater awareness of diversity: of gender, learning styles, interests, aspirations, simple levels of literacy and numeracy and even very occasionally ethnicity.

We weren't very sophisticated judges of teaching quality. If it wasn't good, we responded with boredom or disobedience. For most of the time, pleasurable moments tended to be those when we did something with our hands – like woodwork or art. But there were also other reactions. Few of us had much insight into our own consciousness and a capacity to reflect on deeper emotions. In my own case, anxiety was getting in the way of learning. This was no more evident than in Form 2 or 3 when confronted with quadratic equations. Mathematical advance would be enhanced enormously if those who taught it understood the mind-freezing, sweating, depressing nature of anxiety. No doubt such insights were too much for the more mathematically competent teachers to understand.

Then there is the value of quadratic equations for students never likely to set the maths world on fire. Would basic statistics be more useful for protecting their finances or understanding claims by politicians or the media? The manipulation of letters and numbers posed by quadratic equations related to nothing I knew in life. If it was part of the foundation for a later career in science or engineering, it was never made apparent to us. Moreover, there is a limit to the extent that far distant reward is a sufficient motivation. While I was fumbling around, going blank, others around me were sitting twiddling their thumbs having long finished the required exercise. I could do mental and written arithmetic problems but went on to fail ignominiously at Leaving (Form 5) Maths 1. Not just once but twice! It looked as if I was never to enter the world of abstract reasoning. It is little consolation that some claim that time spent rote learning times tables, as we had done, paves the way for concentration on more cognitively challenging tasks. I had done the paving but was never to gain an understanding of the architecture of mathematics that was the presumed destination. Doubtless there were other times in school when anxiety took over that I simply suppressed in the interests of protecting a fragile ego.

By any stretch of the imagination, boys held a privileged place in secondary school. They disrupted classes and initiated more subversive behaviour beyond the classroom, and they claimed more space in the school ground. It was boys who felt entitled to speak their mind and I was as culpable as any. While girls were observant, they remained silent. When a male teacher stood at the edge of the quadrangle, hands in pocket and scratching between his legs, it was a boy, an Ouyen kid who asked, 'Who's winning, sir?' – this a reference understood by all familiar with the term 'pocket billiards'. It was a culture in which the very capable ones learnt to conceal their talents, and especially if they were girls.

Ralph was doubly disadvantaged. Although male, he did not move like a sportsman or show interest in footy, cricket or tennis. Worse, his abiding interest was maths and physics and he was very good at them.

A lot of life was clearly about winning and losing. It was functional on the football field or when cutting off a shot at the tennis net but in the hierarchy of life where there were always others of superior talent. It was not a recipe for contentment. Even so, one might have concluded from the examination practices that it was. It too readily led me to make invidious comparisons between my meagre abilities and those of someone else. It was most unnerving when they resided in someone who lived nearby and whose company I had to keep almost daily. This was the situation with David and our riding our bikes in search of our cows. This sense of congenital inferiority surely pushed me into regular exercise from the age of fourteen. I figured I would have a better chance of defending myself against some imagined foe – and vainly, even looking better – if I were fit and strong. No bully was going to kick beach sand in my eyes as the Don Athaldo brochure advertising exercise springs claimed.

Such a preoccupation was encouraged in a very physical culture whether in the paddocks or on the sports field, the centre of much social life. It was a value set which contributed to country towns contributing disproportionately to the composition of elite urban sporting teams. My tendency to compare myself unfavourably with others was brought to the fore in that match when we played Tempy. Did the Walpeup selectors have to make such a point of my placement against someone, younger than I was, who was so good that he eventually represented Victoria twice in interstate Aussie rules football?

One classmate who exemplified exceptional natural ability was Paul, but happily an early friendship with him and the fact that his talents greatly exceeded mine made his achievements acceptable. For once, I managed to avoid making self-debasing invidious comparisons. On top of his being awarded an instructor's certificate in swimming when I was splashing around trying to swim to the other side of the pool for my *Herald* Learn to Swim certificate, he was a more than competent diver. To be fair, in Walpeup, there was neither the facility for swimming nor experience of vital early coaching. He could also flash down a 100-yard track in about ten seconds, not far behind times being recorded by the then Australian champion, Hector Hogan.

Running fast was like breathing to Paul. He and I were once among competitors in an 880-yard race. At the time, I was undoubtedly fit and very briefly, on an inside lane, leading the field. Soon, I heard his rhythmic pounding as he drew rapidly up behind me. As he whizzed past to head up the strait, the turbulence nearly knocked me off balance. I was left to watch his relentless flight to the tape, high arm swing, shoulders square, body firm, feet digging into the turf. Interestingly, he took all of this lightly. He could seemingly succeed at anything. In no time, he learnt how to use a trumpet mouthpiece.

We once went on holiday together in Sandringham where, memorably, the proprietor of the hotel, sitting upright at a table, called out, 'My tea, Anna, my tea!' like a member of an English class system. Down on the beach, Paul, armed with sketchbook, captured in a few deft strokes the unsteady waddle of a two-year-old toddler making his way along the sand. It was a depiction worthy of a Toulouse Lautrec.

For all this, my friend was not a great scholar and had to face failure later at school. Too many skills? Too many options? Disdain for the dull grind of study? Could the school have made better use of his multiple talents?

Learning at school was mostly about mastering and absorbing what was foreign to us. Occasionally we engineered distraction through pranks or by diverting Mr Hownslow away from Form 2 and 3 French language into talks about his bicycle trips around Europe. The effects of our conniving was that we knew little of the language by Fourth Form. Confronted by our ignorance, Mr Kelly raised his hand to his forehead in mock horror. '*Nom de Dieu! Sacre Bleu!*' he uttered with a half-smile. He did so relishing the challenge of patiently developing in us a liking for the subject and a willingness to undergo the discipline to achieve some mastery. Nightly homework of vocabulary, verbs conjugated with *être*, adjectives preceding the noun – both learned with rhyming mnemonics – and a stiff dose of prose and translation exercises, all these we accepted as the path to success and satisfaction. Still fair game for a nickname, however. He had protruding ears and wore his black hair smoothed down over the back of his head so that from the rear, we likened him to a 'Volkswagen with the doors open'. He had enough self-assurance to tolerate a bit of fun we engineered and saw its motivating potential. To learn the poetry required for external Leaving (Year 11) and Matriculation exams we used a wind-up record player. We thought that Paul Verlaine's *Chant d'Automne* would be improved a bit if we just stopped winding it. The result was '*Les sanglots longs des violons de l'automne blessent mon coeur d'une langeur montone*' became a slow, descending guttural sound like a weary bass baritone singing a dirge through a drainpipe.

Noted American psychologist and educator, John Dewey, who advocated democracy in schooling and learning by doing and engagement, died in 1951, my second year. We could have benefited from a bit of Deweyism, because our school's faith in chalk and talk was unassailable. Huck Trice, leather jacket, raspy voice and stained smoker's teeth that he habitually revealed in an infectious laugh, did his bit in Third Form to illustrate the wisdom of Dewey. Huck had laboured at home with a surprising level of persistence to make a Ned Kelly suit of metal armour and was determined we should use it in class. We therefore conjured up a Glenrowan siege out in the yard for our star performer. Sheer force of personality by someone not noted for his commitment to scholarship thus led teacher Doug Cavendish to relent and depart from chalk and talk. For once, a history lesson was fun. Even in our Matriculation year, in the study of Modern History about the Renaissance and Reformation, the chalk part faded and it was all talk. It struck me also that labelling it Modern History was a bit of a stretch. The teacher, dictated notes he had devised from his reading of the only copy of a particular text available. He did his best but historical research for us students remained a foreign concept.

Curiosity was a quality left languishing back in our infancy. Even Fourth Form General Science A consisted of plodding through experiments in a bogus simulation of the supposed reality of the scientist's laboratory. Julius Sumner Miller's TV program *Why is it So?*

was not to come until years later with the advent of TV. Its theme was that knowledge came from asking questions not handing down received wisdom. Instead, we put a .22 live round in the cast-iron classroom heater and waited expectantly as it did explosive circuits of the inside.

School involved a manifest obedience to rules, and the more rigid the rules, the more they had to be tested. Very early, I seemed to be determined to be on the wrong side of authority. The most charitable interpretation is that it was a route to healthy adult scepticism and unwillingness to take the word of powerful figures on trust.

In Form 1, Mr Cavendish taught us History, including bits about ancient Egypt – potentially absorbing if he had simulated a bit of forensic pathology, delving into mummy embalming techniques, for example, and not just their abstract belief systems and their funny profile drawings. Cavendish was not by nature a tyrant. He cut a heroic image, standing with left hand brought thoughtfully to his cheek, golden chain dangling from his wrist. Not many farmers wore golden wrist chains at the time. Formerly an Anglican, he had recently converted to Catholicism and there is none so zealous as the convert. Little bits of Catholic doctrine and ritual somehow found their way into his lessons to a bunch of kids much more focused on practical matters. He wrote clearly on the blackboard, but simply too much. 'Learning' consisted of our feverishly copying such notes into our books, a task usually impossible before the recess-time bell and the chance to head down the hill to kick the footy. What is worse, in continuing to write until the last minute, his large frame obscured the blackboard.

Sitting down near the back, I called out, 'Would you mind removing your carcass please, sir? I can't see,' as if such a request was the entitlement of an eleven-year-old.

Left hand clenched, redness surging up his neck into his face, his lips moved but no words came out. Finally, he just told me not to be cheeky. The sniggers from fellow students suggested that the score was

BH one, Cavendish zero. Regrettably, it was the first offence in what became several years of recidivism.

In most classrooms, when notes were copied from the blackboard, conversation was forbidden. Collaborative group work was unheard of. Whether this same DC remembered the earlier incident or not – for I was now twelve – it is understandable that a teacher would not forget such brazen impudence, even if no dossier of recalcitrants was kept in the staffroom. Extraversion, insecurity, reaction to perceived repression – whatever the reason, I continued to talk in class and apparently did not heed a warning to desist.

'Would you like me to thrash you, Hampel?' said the same teacher, now shaking with impotence.

I guessed there was more intention than question in this. Nevertheless, 'I'm not particular, sir,' I said, taking a punt that he would not follow through with his threat.

The exasperated teacher was left with no recourse but to honour his promise. He ordered me to 'Come out here!' and stand in front of the class, who were now watching proceedings in uneasy silence.

Some of them, weary at my antics shuffled with loyalty-testing anxiety or anger. I think they felt I'd gone too far. Defiance not an option, I clattered my way out of my desk and approached the platform.

It should be noted that the only purpose of the desk on the raised platform at the front of the class appeared to be to provide a home for the strap in its drawer. This disciplinary aid was a piece of black leather about eight millimetres thick, three centimetres wide and forty-five centimetres long. In a bit of unfortunate play acting during a lunch hour, one of the kids had brought it down on the desk with a nerve-gripping whack! It should have been salutary. In the right hands, this weapon clearly could inflict searing pain but we had talked about minimising its effect. Always ensuring the blow struck across the hand rather than up the wrist was one of them. Dropping the hand down, like catching a speeding cricket ball, only risked provoking extra blows and was therefore not favoured.

By this time, lips quivering with righteous anger, his face reddening,

DC barked, 'Raise your hand! Higher!' He lifted the strap high and bent his upper body forward with each downward stroke to give added force, three times on the left and twice on the right.

Why not three on the right? Why did I not receive the traditional six of the best? (I could not imagine what six of the worst would be like.) I don't think he had worried about my being right-handed and therefore unable to copy down notes but did he fear class sympathy if I began crying? My hands began to sting unbearably and it was a matter of honour not to let the tears welling up break out on my cheeks as I walked with strained nonchalance back to my seat.

'Back to work!' meaning, 'Copy down these notes!'

There was a discomforting silence. Furtive glances spread across the now silent room, kids assessing the situation. Some, I believe, saw an act of weakness, an ineffective response to a professional challenge.

Cavendish simply lost control. At other times, the lack of harshness in his voice and occasional reluctant laughter confirmed to us the presence of another person inside. Perhaps a desire to be liked led to chinks in his authority, occasions when we took advantage of him. One occurred during a lunch hour the following year. I and other bus travellers had just finished our sandwiches when an opportunity presented itself. This teacher with whom I had developed a special relationship, on lunch duty at the time, chose to go to the toilet. No press-button flush, ceramic washbasins or hand dryers. This was chain flushers behind a limestone extension of the woodwork block. It had a heavy external door of thick vertical planks painted in green. Unfortunately for DC, there was also a stout bolt lock on the outside. Unless there was fear of marauding toilet bowl vandals, or toilet paper thieves, it was difficult to see the purpose of such a lock. Murphy saw his chance. Glancing quickly back for approval from the half dozen boys now wide-eyed at the prospect of a bit of fun, he quietly sidled up and slid the bolt home.

Cavendish came out of the cubicle. 'Whoever it was, open the door!'

'What's wrong, sir? Don't you like it in there?'

Boys now gathered in a semicircle, feet astride, determined not to miss the spectacle.

'Open this door!'

At this point, Robbo started a chant and the rest of us quickly joined in. 'Three old maids were locked in the lavatory. They were there from Sunday to Saturday but nobody knew they were there.'

As we began the reprise, DC relented. 'Come on. Open the door. You've had your fun.'

At the teacher's apparent admission of defeat, Murphy moved forward with an 'Are you sure, sir?' He paused and slid the bolt back.

With that, the hapless teacher strode down to the staffroom in silence and we went to kick the footy.

Given the maxim that whatever you spend most time at, you generally become good at, as a cohort, we were better at sport than scholarship. Scholastics brought neither great interest nor achievement for the bulk of kids. Perversely, although I was quite good at football, tennis, running and throwing, I was no match for some of the boys, who were simply outstanding. This possibly led me to direct some energy into study during the last two years of high school.

Between 1950 and 1955, homosexuality was never perceived, never discussed and never the cause of overt discrimination in our school. We lived masculine, physical, non-reflective lives, most of us happily bathed in a sporting culture. We did notice the way DC walked – most unlike that of ex-Prime Minister Abbott. Along with his hand gestures, we saw him as effeminate. Our attacks – our one day rolling him in the grass, pulling large tufts and stuffing them down his back – were surely evidence of a form of misogynistic pack mentality and, to an extent, a mild *Lord of the Flies* attack on the vulnerable. To his credit, he tolerated this conduct in a way few would have done. The fact that I joined in this later innocent bit of skylarking suggested I harboured no resentment at the public flogging I received at his hands. Perhaps it occurred in the context of my feeling at home and in the community that I had no cause to feel aggrieved and had to accept that I had been a bit of an idiot.

The distribution of teachers, meagre resources, and timetabling decisions – these were some of the things that made school either enjoyable or barely tolerable. Was it an unprecedented act of thoughtfulness or just sheer luck that led woodwork (no longer called Sloyd) to be timetabled on Monday morning, nine a.m. to lunch hour? Unlike practice in other classes, we were permitted to talk in woodwork, even if at times it was just to ask for the persuader (a hammer) when a screw failed to do the right thing. Most importantly we could analyse and dissect Saturday's football matches to the last kick and last goal. Thanks to the operation of buses coming from towns in several directions, all teams were spoken for. It was good to work with our hands in woodwork even if the precision required for a dovetail joint was a challenge for me. By contrast, a less fortuitous positioning of classes was placing a period for an analysis of Shakespeare's *Richard II* immediately before Friday afternoon's sport.

Despite the fact that teacher Mr Arch Arbuthnot ominously inscribed 'Flagellator' on a piece of wood seventy centimetres by seven centimetres by eight millimetres that he hung by the door of the woodwork centre, his reign was not absolute. Occasionally, he was guilty of overreach and picked on the only fat kid in the class. Fat Macka was not a trouble-maker, his crime apparently no more than querying a teacher edict. To us bystanders, it seemed that our teacher was venting frustration at a failure to better manage the other cheekier members of class. No flogging stool or nineteenth-century triangular rack, the offender had to bend double, put his head in a bottom cupboard and be whacked on the backside. With Fat Macka, Mr A couldn't miss. The punishment over, the red-faced kid emerged like a big Friesian backing out of a milking stall, dust now covering his head and shoulders, to looks of silent disapproval from fellow class members.

In addition to this incident, Mr A's demeanour didn't endear himself to us. As he spoke, he turned his head on one side, narrowed his eyes and squeezed out his words with a nasal twang. To me it suggested cynicism and hostility.

Humiliation can take many forms and what followed soon after was retaliation by any measure. Raised off the ground, the woodwork centre had a large space under the floor, accessible by manhole. For some reason, our teacher had to go to the main building. Immediately he left, Victor suggested we all disappear down below. Although in other respects reluctant to submit to discipline, we acted as one, and gathered under the classroom, no one uttering a sound. Arch poked his head in the door, muttering to himself about his vanished class. Assuming we had hidden outside somewhere, he left again, allowing us to all come up from below. Unfortunately, the last one was still emerging like an errant Orpheus when he returned. It is hard to devise satisfactory punishment for an entire class because, when shared, it ceases to be punishment.

Woodwork and metalwork classes were a godsend for pranks. Arch was a practising artist and, to his credit, tried to encourage creativity in his charges. It seemed like a good idea at the time to order a large container of sculptor's clay which he stored in the sheet-metal room. This was not the occasion for Michelangelo's successor to be revealed but, arguably, the motivation was laudable. Unfortunately, the capacity to mould clay into missiles and an endemic liking for throwing meant that as soon as Arch took another unwise trip outside, warfare broke out. Very soon we realised that opponents sheltering below the level of benches could still be attacked if we aimed a large wad of clay at one of the Primus stoves above them on the bench. Once hit, it tumbled down on the crouching kid's head. There were several of these devices on which several soldiering irons could be heated at once. After this brief but exciting diversion from soldering serviette rings and bashing out ashtrays, the tub of clay was quietly locked in a back storage space.

Perhaps there was after all a dossier of trouble-makers kept in the staffroom which Arch also found useful. In Form 3 Art, his exasperation with my indiscipline grew daily until he decided that shame might work. He made me stand on a desk while classmates continued with their quiet work behind easels that he had introduced. Most of the class were now hidden behind them. Again the idea was laudable but rather than encouraging creativity or the feeling that we were real artists, it simply increased insubordination. Arch seemed to gain little satisfaction with the new form of control he exerted over me but come time to issue results for Art, there was evidence of revenge. My fifty per cent mark seemed a little harsh for one in whose home hung the works of an uncle artist talented enough to make Ballarat Gallery and the Queen's private collection. That was my assessment of the injustice at the time anyway. I ignored the fact that talent can skip a generation.

I can only speculate on Arch's feelings when his Matriculation class now consisted of two, one of whom had caused him no end of frustration earlier. Still, to his credit, in the face of my obvious lack of artistic ability, he encouraged me to try all sorts of media: watercolours, powder paints, chalk, and even etching. The trouble was I could not resist the challenge of the heavy-based press with the enormous winding handle on top used to print the etchings. A clear invitation for me to test my strength. A loud crack signalled the end of that particular activity, for the upper plate of the press cracked in half. Miraculously, I did pass the external exam, probably because History of Art's appeal pushed me over the line. Early, I felt the Greeks had it right in promoting the concept of healthy mind in healthy body. I ignored the fact that harbouring lofty and sanctimonious ideals like this was surely setting me up for boring people stupid. Myron's famous statue *Discobolus* (the discus thrower) inspired me to try my hand at it, not realising that until I watched how effortlessly star footballer Curly could hurl the discus out of sight, there was such a thing as natural aptitude and I didn't have it.

School reports were brief and if they were to carry any weight with a future employer, I would have been assured of long-term unemployment. The sum total of my year's work in Third Form (Year 9) was recorded in these memorable lines. 'Bill could have been of more help in class in some subjects.' That was it; just twelve words. At least the form teacher who wrote it knew the meaning of euphemism.

This might have been an appropriate assessment of my behaviour but my school results apart from Third Form Art were reasonable throughout the year. Like the golfer whose self-esteem depends on the one time when the ball clicked off his driver and disappeared towards the hole, I draw on my Fourth Form Arithmetic. Having travelled overseas for most of the term, I still managed best mark for that subject. Not Maths. From Form Two, Maths might as well have been Swahili. Australian History in the manner taught bored me – and not only because Aboriginal history was erased – so I confined my study to the other eight subjects, which I passed. I was awarded twelve per cent for history – probably for signing my name.

Despite the previous visit from the local plod and the stern warning from Dad, I could not kick the stone-throwing habit, this time aiming at railway fittings as I walked from school to Ouyen streets in pursuit of a Volk's pie. Despite the anticipated mouth-watering pleasure awaiting me, I could not ignore a bit of recreational throwing. By this time, I was fourteen and in Fourth Form (Year 10). Ambrose Douglas, the principal, was cut from a different cloth. Instead of giving me yet another hand-searing series of the cuts, he did a bit of strategic thinking. Public thrashing and the desired humiliation clearly hadn't worked. This time words did, even though to this point the visit from Plod for my insulator-smashing rampage hadn't been very successful. Ambrose had enough faith in his reformative powers to offer me next year, the position of head prefect in an admittedly extremely small field. I refused on the grounds of my youth. A scintilla of doubt about my own transformation perhaps? In Sixth Form, I relented and accepted the offer. Nothing is surer than to come first or second in a two-horse race.

A frequent question asked on talkback radio is, 'Who was your favourite teacher?' Callers respond at length about the one 'who opened my mind to the wonders of science', or 'Miss Kfoops who wakened my love of literature', and so on. I should be grateful to Mr Douglas, who suggested to me there were alternatives to being a complete idiot. (I am reminded of a line from an ABC radio comedy years ago when Joe asks his friend, 'In what sense, Charlie, are you not a *complete* idiot?')

The tenor of my previous assessment of my teachers is perhaps unkind. There were a number of positives and at no stage did I ever contemplate leaving school. The discipline instilled by the French teacher with the unfortunately shaped head and Tony Abbot ears promoted an enduring liking for French and the romance of the culture. I respected him and this transferred to the subject. As kids, we were more prepared to forgive DC and Arch, despite their resort to violence. We could see a kindlier side and an attempt to create genuine educational opportunities.

What I could not and would not forgive was Mr Lawrence, the bespectacled pocket billiard player, who marched into his first class and wrote Lawrence with a 'That is my name. Learn it!' Making no secret of his being the possessor of an Honours degree, he berated and belittled those in class who had difficulty with grammar. I was generally not one of them but, like Brendan who had lost the fight to my friend with the punchball, I developed an extreme dislike for the man. At a school reunion twenty years later, the first words Brendan uttered with lips pursed and fists clenched, 'That bloody Lawrence. I'd like to meet him in the street on a dark night!' So much for Miss Kfoops.

For the most part, my high school teachers were well intentioned. Some had an easy ride. Mr Bansgrove, for example, English teacher won points in my Matriculation year when he told us of his times as a university bantamweight boxer. I welcomed his informal manner. I also liked doing the exercises on word meanings that he set. Mr Robinson brought the reputation of being a good footballer whose legacy of playing was a seriously injured leg, but above all, he didn't take himself too seriously either. Others went much further. Each year, Mr French took the Leaving (Year 11) class to his house opposite the school for afternoon tea. For discipline purposes, he relied on a penetrating look. Even Mrs Rodda, our first music teacher, genuinely wanted to promote some appreciation of this aspect of our cultural heritage. The trouble is that, much as I genuinely liked Tchaikovsky's *Nutcracker Suite* played on a gramophone, it would have been good occasionally to try one or two other composers in a year of music lessons.

For Intermediate, Leaving and Matriculation, external examination papers progressed from yellow, to green and finally pink. The signal to unfold our long exam papers usually brought a mixture of excitement and anxiety. Had more of the forty-four we started with in 1950 remained, there might have been a better learning environment and capacity to tackle our exams. The pleasure and success of collaborative effort was denied. I was grateful that completing French prose and translation exercises offered regular challenge and some continuing success and satisfaction. In my senior years, I completed these and other homework alone on a large table in a room vacated by my late grandmother.

We had little coaching in exam technique, including constructing an essay, much less one prepared by the teacher on the basis of questions predicted by past papers. Foreign too was the technique of adapting what one knew to an unexpected question. Nor had any student matriculated before me to provide useful insights. Even so, initial nerves under control, writing an exam could be mildly satisfying. Oral exams were another matter. Engaging in a rudimentary and unpractised conversation in French with Miss Willcox from Melbourne University was not my idea of fun no matter how much I had come to enjoy the subject. Tall, formal, she did her best to put me at ease. Despite all this, at the end of my final year, I was grateful to receive a telegram from my older sister: 'Congratulations. Pass in all subjects. Love, Neta.'

Schooling for some can undoubtedly be stressful. Never pushed by my parents and only focused on not ending up prematurely married or sinking into alcoholism, I settled for the minimum goal of getting out. Stress therefore did not come from competing with others – or striving to achieve the stellar results required for a good job. Teaching and nursing seemed to be the main models among the lesser professions and somewhere along the line, despite no great urging from the teachers I had experienced, I settled on university training for secondary teaching. This took more than a minimum of self-delusion because in Form 4, a vocational guidance test had concluded after all that I was on the borderline for university success. My excuse was that I wasn't smart enough to understand the testing game. Thrown by one of the non-verbal items, I didn't think to simply go on to the next. There were time limits after all. Still, I was to learn that persistence could be a helpful attribute. One bright light shining from afar was when a visiting geography inspector suggested he would get me into Melbourne High if I failed my Matriculation exam at the first try. For some, that was expected practice. I believed it was an academically selective school so I thought it best not to enquire too deeply into how my entry into such a hallowed institution was going to be achieved. Fortunately, I did not fail and did not have to get in under the radar.

It is true that my doggedness and willingness to flog away at French translations laid the groundwork for learning. But it would be churlish in the extreme to deny my secondary school teachers credit for my continued ability to pass examinations and mostly score near best marks in a very, very small pool. Almost universally, they tried. I wish that I could have rewarded the principal who taught us Leaving mathematics but my inability to think through the problems had deep roots. Did I enjoy school? Enjoyment? Satisfaction? Excitement? Yes, some sense of achievement but mostly it was something I just did.

Who would have thought?

My schooling did not kill a desire for academic study. But there was a twist. Who should be offered as a university supervisor in 1980 when I proposed doing a Master's degree? Yes, Doug Cavendish, by now Dr Cavendish, the teacher who, nearly thirty years before, gave me five cuts. When we met, no mention was made of the cuts, our locking him in the toilet and stuffing grass down his neck. Fortunately, his scholarly interests did not coincide with mine and I moved on. Ultimately, I sought out a professor whose work I respected for my doctorate supervisor. Graciously, she always saw herself as just one of many sources of knowledge.

Another, less ambiguous legacy of a bush childhood is my enduring concern for trees, birds, mammals, reptiles, invertebrates – all our ecosystem, in fact – and the climate change so clearly and irrevocably damaging it. It prompted me to interview and write about fourteen farmers who respect climate science and who have significantly changed their practices. Three of them absorb more carbon than they produce. Quite an achievement for farmers raising livestock, the major source of agricultural methane, a major greenhouse gas. (*Against the Grain*, Rosenberg, 2015.)

Epilogue

It's late December 2018, sixty-two years since I left Walpeup, my childhood home. Brother Bruce and I decide to visit for a day and we head first out to the recreation reserve. For me, it was a Saturday footy ground where I played for the Firsts, but there was also girls' netball and an annual community fair. Now, before us, an expanse of grey, tussocky grass and a few struggling shrubs in a clearing among the pines. Goalposts, boundary fence and dressing shed are gone. Even the galvanised-iron toilets are no longer, probably salvaged for someone's chook house. Instead of car horns triumphantly tooting a Walpeup goal, a crow's mournful, elongated 'caark caark' echoes across the emptiness.

We circle around to where the Mallee Research Station officers conducted field days and encouraged farmers to adopt new breeds of wheat and use different soil management techniques. Closed some time ago, I heard. Now, there are big, newish buildings, designed for accommodation and meetings, but no evidence they're being used. All about, in sheds and on the ground, machinery lies abandoned and rusting.

Back towards town but still over the railway line from the main street, a small bare patch in scrub marks the site of the three gypsum tennis courts. Indignant, I feel it's a kind of theft, an attempt to remove the past. But it cannot erase memories of summers I spent playing countless absorbing games of singles, of Easter tournaments, and players from as far as Mildura, and cool soft drink for us ballboys.

Crossing the rail, an entire railway community has vanished: station razed, platform levelled, three railway residences and goods shed demolished. Nothing to hit a tennis ball against now. The silo still stands. They say its machinery was too slow to handle bigger volumes of grain. But, too big and solid to remove, it stands defiant. It's all bulk storage in the Mallee now. Huge piles of grain under coloured tarpaulins wait for favourable prices. No longer carted by rail, it's hauled down south in semi-trailer trucks.

It doesn't pay to go back to the tiny town of one's childhood, especially after such a long time. Memories have lasted but buildings haven't. So much that helped to mould our identities has disappeared. Where once cars lined the street every Saturday morning, there is now only one shop, and that survives with community help. Once there were four shopkeepers: Mr Lyell, Miss Schubert, Mrs Dickie and Mr Sly the butcher. Every Saturday morning, farmers' cars lined the street. But during the week, a car passing through towards Pinnaroo or Ouyen was a notable event because Walpeup was both isolated and self-sufficient. Now, the main street – the highway – carries a bit of through traffic. Admittedly, our visit is in late December – holiday season. Bigger centres like Red Cliffs and Mildura have been brought closer because bitumen roads have replaced gravel. I suspect that most of the entertainment comes to town via television. Nothing peculiar to Walpeup about that of course. That these developments are trends does not lessen the sadness of this return visit.

On the way up north, we stop in Ouyen and glance at the sign in a real estate agent's window.

For Sale
13 Cregan Street Walpeup, Victoria
Price: $72,000–$78,000

'A Hidden Gem in the Country', it says.

That's our place! We moved into it from the more modest house, also a weatherboard one, two doors up the street. Now, the ad reads, 'renovated bathroom and modern shower' and 'downlights throughout'. In the early 1950s, we had no shower but a bath with chip hot water heater and lights dangling from the ceiling. Clearly, with that price, Walpeup is no Melbourne or Sydney but word is that other houses have been sold recently. Some sort of revival apparently but based on what? Affordable housing? Distant employment? But, Mildura and Red Cliffs are still 120 kilometres away. At least I'm glad the ad shows that our house is now more liveable and it's still occupied.

Incongruously, a motorbike sits in the bare, unlit window of Mr Lyell's brick shop. I can still see him: curly black hair, glasses high on his forehead, standing in his white apron behind the long wooden counter. Up the street, the bank's concrete steps where Lacey and I read *Blackhawk* comics on Sunday morning are still there, but along the building's wall, bare boards appear beneath curled remnants of paint. McCracken's bakery is long gone, and next door, land is vacant where Mrs Dickie's shop stood. Locals tell me it burnt down in 1953. Surely I would remember that, as I do Bertie Corbett's house fire earlier on. I was overseas for a while in '53. Perhaps that explains it.

So far, sadly, human hands have removed more of the town than fire, not wantonly, but in response to wider economic forces. If any building was the cultural centre of town it was the Memorial Hall, still standing in its familiar red brick. Community singing, Anzac services, dances and, briefly, attempts to promote table tennis: the hall meant a lot to us. I wonder if today there are any perspiring four-year-old Seven Dwarfs marching offstage with crêpe paper leaking colour down their faces. A few years ago, local women patiently wove a tapestry depicting farming scenes which now hangs in the hall. Word is that there is to be a dance on New Year's Eve, but will enough come?

Up the hill further, also red brick, the Catholic church has been bought and its owner uses it as a storeroom. At least it has survived physically if not spiritually, unlike the neighbouring Church of England. Even the patched-up water tanks opposite, that stood high and black against the blue sky on their big knotted poles, are gone. No more refreshing shower from their thin veil of leaking water as you pass. They were far more interesting than the smaller, squat rectangular metal tank that is there now.

On the other side of the plantation, the primary school we attended I see was tarted up: painted, play equipment, and a classroom transported from neighbouring Torrita, the sign says. But the school no longer operates. Enrolments fell and remaining parents preferred the bus trip to Ouyen. No doubt the school's stables were dismantled long before. At least the currajong tree thrives behind where the goalposts were. It is unusually green, unlike the sugar gums around the edge that Bruce and I dutifully watered over summer holidays. Most of them have died.

We drive down the hill and take the signed turn-off to the tip, our progress soon halted by a forbiddingly high mesh fence and locked gate. Instead of simply discarding rubbish at whim, residents are now confronted by a large board displaying an array of dumping charges that, for bigger loads, would make anyone think twice. To the left, along a familiar track winding through the scrub, rusty tins lie randomly like archaeological relics of an ancient culture.

Back in town and down the hill from the water tank, the Presbyterian church has gone. But in the scrub opposite, is the former Methodist church, still made of cement sheet but as a 'Uniting/ Community Centre', it has moved with the times.

In this arid climate, water meant so much to the town. Like explorers of old, we went on a search for dams. The two at the bottom of town receiving water from the Grampians – or is it the Murray – still function, or at least have water. Try as we did, we could not find Pigeon Tank dam along the mail run where Bruce remembers catching yabbies. Like the tadpole dam not far out north and the bigger 'government' one where I caught redfin, it remained hidden from us, somewhere behind a screen of protective scrub.

We realise as we're about to leave that we've not gone down to Walpeup Lake. Perhaps a good thing because it no longer has water and, unpopularly to some, me included, exotic willows replaced native pines and eucalypts along its margin.

It would be an injustice to Walpeup its residents to ignore the positives. Despite being a grim reminder of so many I knew, the cemetery just north of town grants them respect. There are obvious signs of care: grass removed and graves clearly marked. The crazy velodrome-steep bend of the road at the railway crossing has been replaced by a new road, a straighter and safer one, direct to Ouyen. Visitors approaching that northern end of town might be enticed to take a nature walk where native shrubs are identified. Travellers can use the toilet block and shower in the little camp ground at the nearest end of the street where a sign tells us a mobile library pulls in. We had no library, remember. At the other end, opposite the silo where the coffee palace stood in the 1940s, there is a quite magnificent native garden – an arboretum, it could legitimately be called. As shown in real estate ads for houses recently sold in Walpeup, many are far more comfortably furnished than those of my childhood. Yet for all this, these changes seem to represent a struggle against superior economic and climatic forces.

As a child, I loved being part of Walpeup's community and it was great to wake to nature's crisp morning chill, the blue skies, the bird life, and then enjoy the stillness as evening gave way to starry nights.

www.ingramcontent.com/pod-product-compliance
Lightning Source LLC
Chambersburg PA
CBHW071827080526
44589CB00012B/938